THE ANCHORED PATH

Rediscovering the Way of Jesus

Paul Durbin

Copyright © 2026 Paul Durbin

All rights reserved

No part of this book may be reproduced, or stored in a retrieval system, or transmitted in any form or by any means, electronic, mechanical, photocopying, recording, or otherwise, without express written permission of the publisher.

ISBN: 9798245314945
Imprint: Independently published

All scripture quotations, unless otherwise indicated, are taken from The Holy Bible, New International Version®, NIV®. Copyright © 1973, 1978, 1984, 2011 by Biblica, Inc. Used with permission of Zondervan. All rights reserved worldwide. www.zondervan.com

Scripture quotations marked (AMP) are taken from the Amplified® Bible, Copyright © 2015 by The Lockman Foundation. Used by permission. www.Lockman.org

Scripture quotations marked (NLT) are taken from the Holy Bible, New Living Translation, copyright ©1996, 2004, 2015 by Tyndale House Foundation. Used by permission of Tyndale House Publishers, Carol Stream, Illinois 60188. All rights reserved.

Scripture quotations marked (ESV) are from The ESV® Bible (The Holy Bible, English Standard Version®), © 2001 by Crossway, a publishing ministry of Good News Publishers. Used by permission. All rights reserved.

Scripture quotations marked (KJV) are from the KING JAMES VERSION, public domain.

Cover design by: Paul Durbin
Library of Congress Control Number: 2018675309
Printed in the United States of America

*To Patty.
What a joy to walk the Anchored Path alongside you.*

We have this hope as an anchor for the soul.

You make known to me the path of life.

HEBREWS 6:19, PSALMS 16:11

CONTENTS

Title Page
Copyright
Dedication
Epigraph
Foreword
Author's Note

1. Rediscovering the Anchored Path	1
ANCHOR ONE: BELONG	10
2. I Have Loved You	11
3. Unconscious on the Road	17
4. Looked at and Loved	27
5. The Clear Teaching	34
6. The Shape of Belonging	41
ANCHOR TWO: BELIEVE	49
7. Four Spiritual Truths	50
8. More Than Sorry	62
9. The Essence of Faith	79
10. The Shape of Believing	93
ANCHOR THREE: BECOME	99

11. The Shape of Becoming	100
12. Buried With Christ	108
13. Raised with Christ	126
ANCHOR FOUR: BELAY	143
14. The Shape of Belaying	144
15. Space at the Table	158
16. Space in Our Conversations	172
17. Space With Our Resources	189
18. Belayed to Belay	205
Appendix A: Belaying and Anchors	209
Appendix B: Listening Prayer	214
Appendix C: Scriptural Declarations	219
Appendix D: Anchored Origins	228
Appendix E: Anchored Stages	232
Acknowledgement	245
About The Author	247
The Anchored Path	249

FOREWORD

By Steve Pike

I'll never forget the day Andy called me and started the conversation with: "Hi, my name is Andy and I think I might be starting a church backwards."

I was intrigued. "Tell me more," I responded.

Andy proceeded to launch into a fascinating story of how his life as a successful business leader had encountered a divine interruption in the form of the tragic death of a young lady in a neighborhood not far from where he lived. He wondered how such an awful thing could happen so close to home.

His curiosity led him to an uncomfortable discovery. This unnecessary death might have been prevented if the neighborhood had a place for kids to go after school. Something like an after-school program.

Andy decided to do something about it. He researched what it would take to start an after-school program. He got buy-in from community leaders, donations and grants to help fund the program, and started serving the kids in the neighborhood with after-school programming every day from 4-6 p.m.

Like Andy, the staffers of the after-school program were followers of Jesus, and although to maintain funding, it was necessary for the program to be faith-neutral, relationships were formed, and some of the young people decided to follow Jesus.

Andy thought the next logical step was to take the kids to church with him, but the first visit to Andy's large church in an affluent suburb did not go well. The cultural gap was insurmountable. Andy realized what the kids needed was a church in their neighborhood. That's when Andy called me to wonder out loud if he might be starting a church backwards.

As I read the manuscript of *The Anchored Path*, I couldn't help but think of Andy's statement— "I think I'm starting a church backwards." Paul Durbin asks us to consider the possibility that we may have been thinking about church backwards. It's a hard question to face. Is it possible that we've been approaching faith from completely the wrong direction? Have we made "believing" the beginning instead of a part of the journey of following Jesus? These are questions worth pondering and responding to as appropriate.

Which reminds me of another story from a friend who was starting a church. Preston felt called to be the catalyst of a new faith community in a city neighborhood.[1] Part of his start-up strategy was simply to stop in for a friendly visit with all the business owners in the neighborhood. His question for each one was "Why did you decide to start your business in this particular community?"

Most gave him a polite answer and quickly moved on to whatever work their business called on them to do. But one owner turned the question back on Preston. "What are you planning to do in our community?"

Preston responded by announcing, "I moved here to start a church."

The shop owner laughed and replied, "You seem like a nice guy and I'd like to save you a lot of heartache. Most people who live in this neighborhood are not religious people. We're not interested in what you're selling. Why don't you go somewhere where people are interested in a new church? We don't want or need one here."

Undaunted, Preston replied, "Is it possible that you and the church have not been properly introduced?"

The shop owner responded, "What do you mean by that?" That question allowed Preston to help the shop owner become aware of things about the church that he did not understand. Over many meals and deep conversations, he became a fan of the idea of the new church.

It is possible that for many readers, *The Anchored Path* will be a proper introduction or re-introduction to the Church and what it means to follow Jesus. If you're a church leader, this book will help you reimagine how you will help yourself and your congregation practically live out the command to make disciples. If you're a follower of Jesus, you may be inspired toward a more robust imagination for what it means to follow Jesus. If you're a seeker of truth, *The Anchored Path* may serve as a fresh introduction to a faith story you thought you already knew.

Ready to be challenged, enlightened, convicted, encouraged, and inspired? Let's go!

Steve Pike

Founder, Next Wave Community[2]

AUTHOR'S NOTE

The stories in this book are true to my experience and memory. In some cases, I have consolidated events or adjusted timelines for clarity and flow. All dialogue has been reconstructed from memory, attempting to capture the essence of what was said rather than providing word-for-word transcripts. To honor the privacy of those mentioned, I have changed the names of individuals throughout this book (except for my immediate family). Place names and identifying details have also been altered or intentionally kept vague. While these changes preserve anonymity, they don't diminish the truth at the heart of each story—that Jesus meets us where we are and leads us along the Anchored Path.

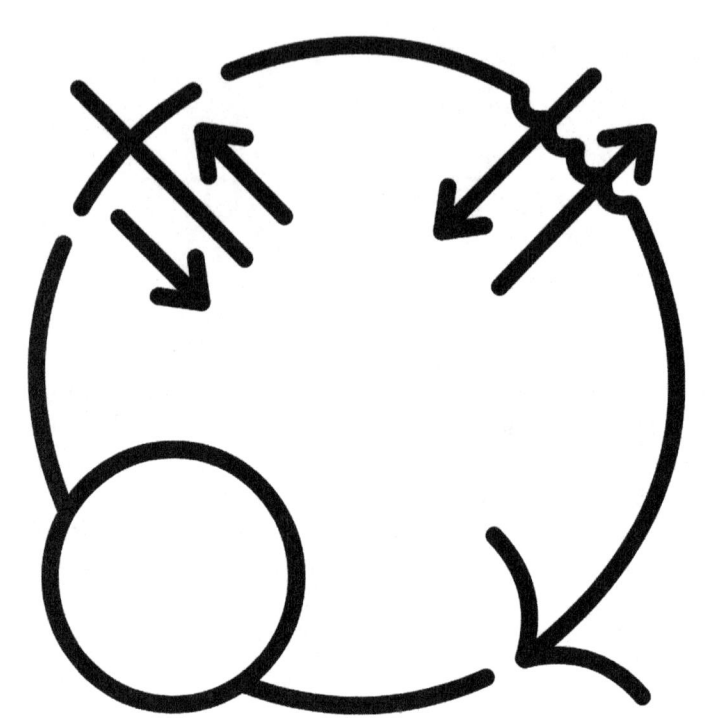

1. REDISCOVERING THE ANCHORED PATH

Stand at the crossroads and look; ask for the ancient paths, ask where the good way is, and walk in it, and you will find rest for your souls. (Jeremiah 6:16)

I've been in church for as long as I can remember.

If I make a conservative estimate—say I've been to Sunday church 40 times a year—then I multiply that by my age (52)—that means I've attended over 2,000 Sunday services.

I've also been to lots of summer Bible camps. Let's say I averaged 1 week of camp per year of my life (again, a conservative estimate). The math works out to 1 year of Bible camp.

Potluck meals? I've sampled more mystery Jell-O salads

than anyone should have to endure.

And as a pastor, I've led a *lot* of this stuff.

I've been a youth pastor, worship pastor, associate pastor, lead pastor, and missionary pastor; and I've done these things in a variety of places: the Midwest, China (the "Middle Country"[3]), and the middle of the Rockies.

And I've noticed something.

Churches and ministers—including me—have often worked from an unspoken and unfortunate formula when it comes to engaging with people.

Before I go any further, I need to say this clearly: I'm sorry.

Sorry for what?

For asking you to walk a path that often looks like this:

Believe → Behave → Belong → Be Seated.

This path can feel uninviting at best—and hurtful at worst. And the truth is, it's not working.

According to a 2021 Gallup poll, U.S. church membership fell below 50% in 2020[4]—down from 70% in 1999. The largest decline was among young adults, with only about 36% of millennials belonging to a church. Similarly, Barna Research found that nearly two-thirds of young adults who grew up in church have dropped out.[5]

Honestly? I don't blame them—or you. Let me explain.

Believe →

1. REDISCOVERING THE ANCHORED PATH

First, we asked you to *believe*. What did we ask you to believe? We asked you to believe in the same way we do.

The comedian Emo Phillips tells this joke:

> Once I saw this guy on a bridge about to jump. I said, "Don't do it!"
>
> He said, "Nobody loves me."
>
> I said, "God loves you. Do you believe in God?"
>
> He said, "Yes."
>
> I said, "Are you a Christian or a Jew?"
>
> He said, "A Christian."
>
> I said, "Me, too! Protestant or Catholic?"
>
> He said, "Protestant."
>
> I said, "Me, too! What franchise?"
>
> He said, "Baptist."
>
> I said, "Me, too! Northern Baptist or Southern Baptist?"
>
> He said, "Northern Baptist."
>
> I said, "Me, too! Northern Conservative Baptist or Northern Liberal Baptist?"
>
> He said, "Northern Conservative Baptist."
>
> I said, "Me too! Northern Conservative Baptist Great Lakes Region or Northern Conservative Baptist Eastern Region?"
>
> He said, "Northern Conservative Baptist Great

Lakes Region."

I said, "Me, too! Northern Conservative Baptist Great Lakes Region Council of 1879, or Northern Conservative Baptist Great Lakes Region Council of 1912?"

He said, "Northern Conservative Baptist Great Lakes Region Council of 1912."

I said, "Die, heretic!" and pushed him over.[6]

Funny, but uncomfortable, because the joke hits too close to home. Love from churches (like mine) and ministers (like me) has often been conditional. Are we "like-minded"? Did you vote for the same candidate? Do you fit in with our kind of people?

Why? Because ensuring you first believed like us made us feel safer. It was love without risks.

Once we established you believed like us, the next step was to let you *belong*, right? Not so fast.

Behave →

We also wanted to see if you behaved like us (on our good days, of course). "Don't do this. Do that. Stay away from them. Stick close to us." After all, if you believed like us, you would instinctively behave like us ... right?

Belong →

Only once we had monitored your belief and behavior long enough to determine you thought and acted like us, could we finally say, "You belong."

Where exactly? In a seat.

Be Seated.

Believe, Behave, Belong, Be Seated. Enjoy the show with people who think and act like you (like us). We turned discipleship into spectatorship, making following Jesus a comfortable show to watch instead of a life to live.

I know we all imagine Jesus differently, but the process I've described above is not at all how the Bible portrays His ministry. When we truly discover Jesus as presented in the Gospels (Matthew, Mark, Luke, and John), we see a more life-giving, ancient path to follow. Instead of a rigid formula, we find four anchors that hold us secure in our journey with Him: Belong → Believe → Become → Belay →

With Jesus, everything starts with the Anchor of Belonging.

Belong →

And by that, I mean His engagement with us starts with love.

In this book, I hope to demonstrate—based on what we see of Jesus in the Gospels—why I believe this. For now, consider this:

> For Jesus, to meet a new person was to love them.
> To see a person was to have compassion for them.

When Jesus invited someone to follow Him, He invited people like us—selfish, full of doubt, carrying a lot of baggage—who didn't believe (at first) that Jesus was who He said He was.

To put it simply, with Jesus:

> People belonged before they believed.
> People were loved before they learned.
> People were shown mercy without merit.

The theological term that describes the heart of Jesus's radical approach is *prevenient grace*. It's grace that precedes any human action, enabling us to freely respond to God's gift of salvation and love.[7]

Believe →

As people grew in their knowledge and trust of Jesus, they began to gravitate toward the Anchor of Believing in Him. For some, that took a while.

For the disciples, it took years! Many of them didn't confess their belief in Jesus until His final hours before the cross. At the Last Supper (which was three years into their relationship with Jesus), they said, "*This* makes us believe that you came from God" (John 16:30, emphasis mine).

To which Jesus replied (and I imagine a slight bit of exasperation in His voice), "Do you *now* believe?" (John 16:31, emphasis mine).

Become →

As the disciples followed Jesus for those three years, He had been gently showing them not just how to behave—

but who to become.

You see, the discipline of behaving (the standard American church way) is about external compliance—following rules and appearing good. In contrast, the Anchor of Becoming (the Jesus way) is about internal transformation—being remade from the inside out.

Being remade to be less hypocritical and more merciful, less fragmented and more whole, less sin-prone and more holy, less foolish and more mature, less selfish and more like He created us to be—like Himself.

Belay →

Throughout this transformation, Jesus kept sending His followers out. Before they fully believed. While they were still becoming. He sent them to:

> Love as He did.
> Do the things He did.
> Testify to the things He had done in their lives.

In other words, Jesus called them to live life—not from a comfortable seat of watching—but in the servant role of belaying.

If you're not from Colorado[8], you may not know: belay is a climbing term. To belay someone is to help them climb by holding the rope, managing the slack, and being ready to catch them if they fall. It's a humble job. You're not the hero. You're not even climbing. You're there to support, to serve.

When you belay, you literally become an anchor point for another person's journey—which makes this the perfect metaphor for our fourth anchor.[9]

In this book, "living on belay" will be our phrase for living on mission with Jesus—to go and lovingly serve and guide others like He did for us.

Our Journey

Here then is the Anchored Path for our journey; we're going to challenge the existing formula:

Believe → Behave → Belong → Be Seated.

And we'll aim to walk along something that might seem new to us, but is actually closer to the way of Jesus:

Belong → Believe → Become → Belay →

Let's start where Jesus started—with the Anchor of Belonging.

Questions For Reflection

1. The path to community in the standard American church is described as Believe, Behave, Belong, Be Seated. Which step in this process has been hardest for you personally? Where have you felt stuck or excluded along this path?

2. Jesus called His disciples to follow Him before they understood who He was or what following Him meant. Think of a time when someone invited you into something before you were "ready" or "qualified." How did that experience shape you?

3. Prevenient grace is described as God's grace that

precedes any human action. What would it mean for your daily life if you truly believed God loves and accepts you before anything you do or don't do?

4. Read the phrase slowly: "You belong before you believe." How does your body react to those words? Do you tense up? Relax? Feel suspicious? Feel relief? What might God be trying to tell you through your reaction?

5. The path metaphor suggests we're all walking somewhere. Where do you feel like you are right now on your spiritual journey—just starting out, somewhere in the middle, feeling lost, or guiding others along their way? What would it look like to take the next step forward?

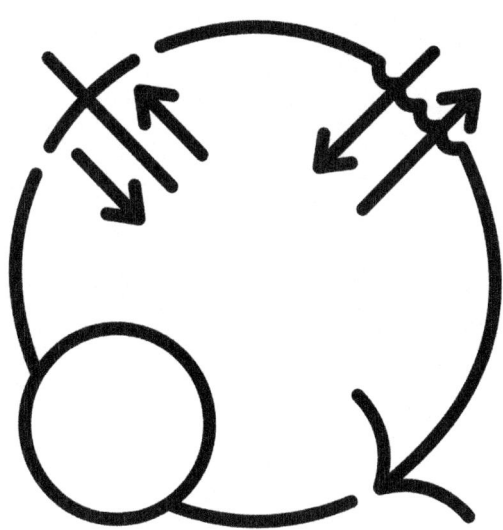

ANCHOR ONE: BELONG

You are the Beloved. I am the Beloved. Every human being is the Beloved of the Lord. – Henri Nouwen[10]

God loves us before he can make anything out of us.[11] – Eugene Peterson

We love him because he first loved us.[12] – Saint John

2. I HAVE LOVED YOU

> *The Lord appeared to us in the past, saying: "I have loved you with an everlasting love; I have drawn you with unfailing kindness." (Jeremiah 31:3)*

How does someone communicate that you belong? Do they just say, "You belong"?

Maybe.

When sincere, those can be powerful words. But do they have to be said explicitly? Or is belonging communicated more clearly through action?

Shingling In The Snow

Let me tell you a story about shingling in the snow.

The first church I led was in North Dakota, where winters can last six months. Luke was part of that church, farming land about forty miles northeast of our community. Besides working his farm, Luke was building a modest house for his wife and two daughters.

Then cancer showed up.

The illness left Luke unable to keep up with his work. Local farmers helped with his fields, and a group of men from our church—myself included—volunteered to finish the roof on his house before winter hit.

The problem? Winter showed up the same day we did. Picture this: six guys on a roof in a whiteout blizzard, shouting to be heard—thirty feet of visibility at best. Far from ideal conditions for shingling a roof.

But shingle we did. By late afternoon—which means pitch dark in North Dakota winter—we had finished.

One of the guys who showed up that day was Henry. He was a man in his late fifties, rough around the edges. Big beard, flannel shirt, suspenders. He once told me he ate raw hamburger from the fridge as a toddler because no one bothered to feed him. He learned early to take care of himself—no one else would.

Henry proudly declared himself president of the local "CAVE Men Club." CAVE stood for Citizens Against Virtually Everything. They met daily at the coffee shop to talk about how bad the world was—and how they could fix it. (This is true. I attended once. I drank really bad café coffee and heard lots of "tea" being spilled).

Some guys from our church had befriended Henry and invited him to help with Luke's roof. What I didn't know was that Henry was watching all of us as we worked. He was definitely pulling his weight, cracking jokes, and making the best of a brutal situation. But he was witnessing something he'd rarely seen: men helping another man out of love.

On The Porch With A Sword

After Luke passed away, Henry showed up at my house the next summer. It was August, one of those perfect late-summer evenings on the front porch.

We made small talk for a bit. Then Henry got serious. He told me how much he loved our church, respected the men there, and respected me. He even said that no matter what, he had my back.

Actually, he said something even more dramatic. Henry told me God had given him a massive sword—a spiritual one, I'm pretty sure—and that he was supposed to use it to protect me and the church. (Relax. That was just Henry's dramatic way of saying he loved and trusted us).

I was surprised. The imagery was fascinating, but more importantly, Henry didn't throw around compliments lightly.

"Why do you feel that way, Henry?"

"You showed up on that roof. People don't do that. They don't shingle houses in a blizzard for free. Especially pastors! When I saw all of you work the entire day and finish the job for that family, I knew I could trust you. You live what you preach."

Humbling. Henry wasn't convinced our church was a place of love and belonging because of my sermons. He was convinced because I showed up on a freezing roof.

Anyone can do that.

To put a finer point on it: Henry didn't become fiercely loyal to our community because someone shook his hand in the church lobby and said, "We love you! You belong here!" Maybe those words *had* been spoken to him— I don't know. But any messages of love that had been spoken didn't land until he was pounding nails in the snow with a group of men.

A Grammar Lesson

This shouldn't have surprised me. Even Jesus didn't have a habit of walking up to people to say, "I love you." Actually—and this might alarm you—Scripture never records Jesus saying those exact words.

Shocking, right?

The closest you'll get is a phrase that almost sounds like it's in the past tense. During the Last Supper, Jesus told His disciples, "I have loved you" (John 15:9). Why did He say it like that? Why not just a simple, "I love you, guys"?

Let's pause for a quick grammar refresher, but first a confession: I like grammar.

I discovered my love for it during my senior year of high school. I took Advanced Grammar from an austere, elderly teacher. I can't remember her name, but Mrs. Sternwood seems appropriate. Despite how seriously she took grammar (or maybe because of it), Mrs. Sternwood kindled in me a love for language.

Now, why the refresher? Because this next bit is pretty amazing: when Bible translators put their minds together to come up with the very best English translation of what Jesus said (in Greek) in John 15:9, they didn't choose past or present tense. They chose the *present perfect tense*.[13]

Why is that so special?

Here's the grammar refresher: the present perfect tense describes an action that started in the past and continues in the present.

Let me repeat that.

> The action started in the past.
> And it continues in the present.

Therefore, the best translation of what Jesus said is not:

> "I love you" (present).
> "I loved you" (past—once upon a time).
> "I will love you" (future—someday).

But rather ...

> "I have loved you" (present perfect—started in the past, continues now).

I Have Loved You

To flesh that out a bit, it wouldn't be wrong to hear Jesus say in this moment, "I have loved you from eternity past, and that love continues in the present."

This sounds a lot like something God said in the Old Testament: "I have loved you (present perfect) with an everlasting love; I have drawn you with unfailing kindness" (Jeremiah 31:3).

Are you catching this?

God's style of love is to demonstrate His love first. To prove it. To show it. Then, He points back to His actions and says, "See? I have loved you."

This is what Henry realized on my porch that summer day. As he looked back at the actions of the men on that snowy roof, he noticed something: we loved Farmer Luke. We even loved Caveman Henry.

And as winter turned to spring, and spring turned to late summer, Henry heard God whispering to him, "See? I have loved you."

Perhaps even now, you can look back and hear Him saying it to you too.

Questions For Reflection

1. Look back over your life like Henry did that summer. Where can you now see evidence of God's love that you might have missed when it was happening?

2. Jesus said "I have loved you" rather than "I love you." How does understanding God's love as both historical and ongoing change how you view your present circumstances?

3. Henry needed to see love in action before words of belonging could land. What "roof moments" in your life —times when Love showed up in work clothes—can help you understand God's love?

3. UNCONSCIOUS ON THE ROAD

> *But a Samaritan, as he traveled, came where the man was; and when he saw him, he took pity on him. He went to him and bandaged his wounds, pouring on oil and wine. Then he put the man on his own donkey, brought him to an inn and took care of him. (Luke 10:33–34)*

Henry woke up to God's love months after that snowy roof. But what if you're still unconscious to God's love? What if He's been loving you all along and you haven't even noticed? This brings us to one of Jesus's more well-known stories.

In the last chapter, we saw how Jesus never explicitly said "I love you" to His disciples—or anyone, for that matter. Instead, He demonstrated His love, then pointed back to His actions to say, "See? I have loved you."

But Jesus did more than demonstrate this kind of love. He also taught it.

Now, Jesus didn't teach like we do. Our western minds prefer an opening thesis, logical flow, a series of points, and a well-designed PowerPoint.

Jesus used stories. More specifically, He used *parables*—stories that used relatable situations to explain deeper, spiritual truths.[14] Entertaining, for sure, but they always had a point (and often a few sub-points woven throughout).

Sometimes, Jesus used items from the animal and plant world—sheep, trees, seeds, bread, fish—to be the "characters" in his parables. Other times, he cast people—farmers, fishermen, travelers, friends—in the lead roles.

But here's the thing about stories: Sometimes we miss an important point because we identify with the wrong character. We think we're the hero when really, we're the one who needs rescuing.

The Good Samaritan

Jesus told a movie-worthy parable that's become known as "The Good Samaritan." Even if you have never cracked open a Bible, you know what it means to be a good Samaritan—someone who helps others in distress without expecting anything in return.

So, I get it. You might be tempted to skip this chapter, thinking, "Good Samaritan, check. I know this one."

Hold on. Being a helper to those in distress isn't the only point. Let's hear the story as Jesus told it in Luke 10:25–37:

3. UNCONSCIOUS ON THE ROAD

On one occasion an expert in the law stood up to test Jesus. "Teacher," he asked, "what must I do to inherit eternal life?"

"What is written in the Law?" he replied. "How do you read it?"

He answered, "'Love the Lord your God with all your heart and with all your soul and with all your strength and with all your mind'; and, 'Love your neighbor as yourself.'"

"You have answered correctly," Jesus replied. "Do this and you will live."

But he wanted to justify himself, so he asked Jesus, "And who is my neighbor?"

In reply Jesus said: "A man was going down from Jerusalem to Jericho, when he was attacked by robbers. They stripped him of his clothes, beat him and went away, leaving him half dead. A priest happened to be going down the same road, and when he saw the man, he passed by on the other side. So too, a Levite, when he came to the place and saw him, passed by on the other side. But a Samaritan, as he traveled, came where the man was; and when he saw him, he took pity on him. He went to him and bandaged his wounds, pouring on oil and wine. Then he put the man on his own donkey, brought him to an inn and took care of him. The next day he took out two denarii and gave them to the innkeeper. 'Look after him,' he said, 'and when I return, I will reimburse you for any extra expense you may have.'"

"Which of these three do you think was a neighbor to the man who fell into the hands of robbers?"

The expert in the law replied, "The one who had mercy on him."

Jesus told him, "Go and do likewise."

The point of the story is "Go and do likewise." Be a good Samaritan. Jesus stated it Himself.

Even without knowing the tension between Samaritans and Jews, we understand that "go and do likewise" means showing compassion to someone who may not have the ability to thank you.

If we stopped there, we'd still have a high bar to live up to.

However, there *was* mutual animosity between Jews and Samaritans, which adds a whole new layer. In the minds of Jesus's original audience, a Samaritan would have been the least likely hero to help a Jewish traveler.

This explains why the expert in the law couldn't even bring himself to say "the Samaritan" when Jesus asked, "Which of these three do you think was a neighbor?" All he could mutter was, "The one who had mercy."

When we're aware of this historical context, we realize Jesus isn't simply commanding compassion. He's commanding us to extend compassion to sworn enemies. People who hate us.

How's that for a high bar?

Plot Twist

And now for a twist. Ready? If you look at the story closer, the character who most resembles the Good Samaritan is ... Jesus.

And the character who most looks like the man on the side of the road is ... us.

I'm not the only one who thinks this. Some of the earliest church leaders—Origen, Clement, Augustine—saw it similarly.[15]

When we read the story that way, we gain a deeper understanding of the love and belonging available to us in Jesus.

Let's consider three aspects of this love:

Love Without Words

I've read this story countless times, but until recently, I never noticed something: There is no recorded dialogue between the Good Samaritan and the injured man. They don't talk! This leads me to assume the man was unconscious, since the robbers left him "half dead."

If the injured man was unconscious, he wouldn't even know he'd been loved until he woke up. He'd been loved without words.

This makes me wonder: How many ways has Jesus wordlessly loved us? What acts of love have we missed while we were unconscious to His presence?

I've heard people ask, "If God is real, why doesn't He just show up? Give me a sign?"

I get it—we want Love to be obvious and unmistakable. Still, I marvel at statements like these. We stand on a planet spinning at 1,000 miles per hour, orbiting the sun at 67,000 miles per hour, and yet we feel none of it. Earth hangs at the perfect distance from the sun—close enough for warmth, far enough to avoid burning. Our atmosphere holds just the right mix of oxygen for life. Plants turn sunlight into food. And the moon? It pulls the tides with such accuracy that entire ecosystems depend on its rhythm.

How's that for love without words?

Remember Farmer Luke? He slept through our work that day, recovering from his treatments while Henry and others pounded nails. He was loved without knowing it. Helped without asking for it. Cared for while unconscious. Loved without words.

Love At Great Cost

The Good Samaritan empties his *own* bank account—not the injured man's—while the man lies unconscious.

>Oil? Not cheap.
>Wine? Not cheap either.
>Two denarii? Two days' wages.

And what about his own life? The Samaritan risked everything on a road known for robbery and violence.

Does that sound familiar?

Jesus walked straight into our mess, our violence, and our rejection knowing exactly what it would cost Him—His life—and exactly what He would accomplish.

The prophet Isaiah foresaw this:

> But he was pierced for our transgressions, he was crushed for our iniquities; the punishment that brought us peace was on him, and by his wounds we are healed. (Isaiah 53:5)

Peter reminded early believers,

> For you know that it was not with perishable things such as silver or gold that you were redeemed from the empty way of life handed down to you from your forefathers, but with the precious blood of Christ, a lamb without blemish or defect. (1 Peter 1:18-19)

And where were we? We were still unconscious on the side of the road. We were still unable to say thanks. We were still His enemies, really.

That's when God's costly love—and His invitation for us to belong—shows up.

Love That Comes Back

Let's keep assuming the injured man is unconscious. He has been beaten by robbers—plural. Outnumbered and unprepared.

He's unaware of the wordless, costly love shown him. He hasn't experienced the shock of who helped him—his enemy, the Samaritan. He hasn't had the chance to say thank you (if his view of Samaritans would even allow it).

But he will get that opportunity. Did you notice what the Samaritan told the innkeeper? "When I return."

The beaten man wasn't loved just enough to be dropped off somewhere. He was loved enough to receive ongoing care.

What a picture of God's love! God keeps showing up. He gives love that is wordless, extravagant, costly—and includes thousands of hours of aftercare.

Yet we reject it.

> Dismiss it.
> Discount it.
> Disregard it.
> Don't even notice it.

We're still unconscious.

But the earth keeps spinning, we keep breathing, and His faithfulness keeps enduring—wordless, costly, ever-present love.

We may never know how the man responded when he finally woke up. But we can know ours. How will you respond when you wake up to this love?

When Belonging Begins

Remember how I said a parable has a point (and often a few sub-points) woven throughout? In this story, Jesus *does* end by stating the primary point: "go and do likewise."[16]

Perhaps you already are *going and doing likewise*. If so, wonderful (and I mean that), but can I ask you just to pause for a moment? Pause just long enough to recognize who *we are* in this story?

We're the unconscious man on the side of the road. We're the ones who have received this wordless, costly love. We're the ones that Love keeps coming back to.

These realizations are more than just sub-points—they're foundational for understanding how God loves us and how belonging actually works.

Belonging doesn't begin when you wake up and recognize who's helping you. It doesn't start when you "go and do likewise."

Belonging begins the moment Love finds you unconscious on the side of the road and decides *you're* worth saving.

Questions For Reflection

1. The injured man was unconscious when Love found him. What does it mean to you that God's love doesn't wait for your permission?

2. What keeps you "unconscious" to God's wordless love? Busyness? Cynicism? Past wounds? Simply never being taught to look for it?

3. The Samaritan promised to return and cover additional costs. How does knowing that God's love keeps coming back—not just a one-time rescue—affect how you view your current struggles?

4. Imagine waking up like the injured man, suddenly aware of all the costly love that has been poured out while you were unconscious. What would it mean for you to truly "wake up" to God's love? What might change?

4. LOOKED AT AND LOVED

Jesus looked at him and loved him. (Mark 10:21)

There's a line from Mark's Gospel that stops me in my tracks every time I read it: "Jesus looked at him and loved him" (Mark 10:21).

Let me show you the whole scene:

> As Jesus started on his way, a man ran up to him and fell on his knees before him. "Good teacher," he asked, "what must I do to inherit eternal life?"
>
> "Why do you call me good?" Jesus answered. "No one is good—except God alone. You know the commandments: 'You shall not murder, you shall not commit adultery, you shall not steal, you shall not give false testimony, you shall not defraud, honor your father and mother.'"

"Teacher," he declared, "all these I have kept since I was a boy."

Jesus looked at him and loved him.

"One thing you lack," he said. "Go, sell everything you have and give to the poor, and you will have treasure in heaven. Then come, follow me."

At this the man's face fell. He went away sad, because he had great wealth. (Mark 10:17–22)

Reflect on this for a moment: before Jesus uncovers the hard truth about this young man's love for his wealth—before the man "went away sad," as Mark puts it—"Jesus looked at him and loved him."

How did Mark even know this? Was it in Jesus's eyes? The warmth in His voice? His body language? Did the young man notice, too?

Mark doesn't answer these questions, but somehow, Jesus's love was so evident that Mark felt compelled to record it. In other words, this love wasn't just something Jesus felt internally—His love was somehow communicated. It was visible, and it was tangible.

I'm struck by how the young man was getting ahead of himself. He wanted to discuss deeply spiritual matters like eternal life—when he hadn't even recognized the embodiment of love standing right in front of him.

If he had truly seen it—really felt what it meant to be loved by Jesus—maybe he would have responded differently to the "sell everything" challenge that followed.

But he missed it. He was so focused on the intricacies of a religious discussion that he overlooked the beauty of a loving relationship.

The Woman Who Expected An Argument

This same pattern shows up repeatedly in Jesus's interactions with people. Take the Samaritan Woman in John's Gospel (John 4:4-36).

It's the middle of the day. Hot. Jesus is tired and thirsty. He sits down by Jacob's well and when a Samaritan woman shows up to draw water, He simply asks, "Will you give me a drink?" (John 4:7).

That's it. No sermon. No confrontation. Just a thirsty Jesus asking for water. But in her shock, she gets a bit defensive: "You are a Jew and I am a Samaritan woman. How can you ask me for a drink?" (John 4:9).

Notice that Jewish-Samaritan animosity, just like in the Good Samaritan story from the previous chapter. She assumes this will be a religious debate. Maybe an argument. Certainly not a normal conversation.

But here's what communicated love before Jesus said the word: He was there. Talking with her. In the heat of the day. Not to argue theology or condemn her sins—even though her life was messy and they both knew it.[17]

He was there for a drink of water and a conversation.

Instead of telling her to clean up her act, Jesus offers something else entirely: "If you knew the gift of God and who it is that asks you for a drink, you would have asked him and he would have given you living water" (John 4:10).

Jesus doesn't start with her failures. He doesn't begin with what she needs to fix. He starts with a gift. With what He wants to give her. With belonging.[18]

Meeting In The Dark

In John's Gospel, Jesus encounters Nicodemus (John 3:1-21).

There are some thorny dynamics here. Nicodemus is a Pharisee, part of the religious establishment growing increasingly skeptical of Jesus. By the social and religious rules of their day, he and Jesus should be adversaries. Or at least keep their distance.

So, Nicodemus comes at night. Under cover of darkness, probably hoping his colleagues won't see him meeting this controversial rabbi named Jesus. And what does Jesus do?

He meets him. At night. On Nicodemus's terms. No public shaming for his cowardice. No demanding he come back in daylight. No "if you really want truth, you'll risk your reputation." Jesus simply meets him where he is.

That's love. That's how Jesus creates belonging—meeting people where they are, not where He would have them to be. And right in the middle of his theological discussion with Nicodemus, Jesus drops what would become the most well-known verse in the Bible: "For God so loved the world that he gave his one and only Son..." (John 3:16).

Even when (or perhaps especially when?) talking theology, Jesus leads with love.[19]

Not Anything-Goes Love

Now, let me be clear about something. This isn't the soft, anything-goes love that our culture often promotes.

Jesus *did* challenge the rich young man to sell everything. He *did* tell the woman at the well to go get her husband, knowing full well she had had five husbands, and her current partner wasn't her husband. He *did* perplex Nicodemus by explaining the need to be born again.

Jesus's love isn't a love that leaves us where we are. It's not inclusive in the way modern culture defines inclusion —where all paths are equally valid and no challenge is given, no change is required.

But—and this is crucial—Jesus's love comes first. *Before* the challenge. *Before* the call to change. *Before* the invitation to believe or live differently.

Please don't get the order wrong.

The rich young man was loved while hearing the hard truth about his possessions. The woman at the well experienced acceptance before Jesus revealed He knew about her troubled past. Nicodemus felt welcomed before being confronted and puzzled by the concept of spiritual rebirth.

The Look That Changes Everything

I keep coming back to that phrase: "Jesus looked at him

and loved him."

What would it mean for you to know—really know—that Jesus looks at you this way? Not after you get your life together. Not once you figure out what you believe. Not when you've demonstrated your worth.

Right now. As you are. With all your questions, doubts, failures, and confusion. Jesus looks at you and loves you.

The question isn't whether you're good enough to belong. The question is whether you'll receive the love that's already being offered. Whether you'll slow down long enough to see that love in His eyes before rushing ahead to the theological debates or moral improvements you think He requires.

Because here's what I'm learning: when we really understand how Jesus looks at people—how He looks at us—everything else falls into place. Belief becomes a response to love, not a requirement for it. Transformation becomes the natural result of belonging, not the cost of entry.

In the next chapter, we'll see that this isn't just how Jesus acted—it's what the Bible explicitly teaches about how God works.

For now, just sit with this: before anything else, before any other conversation, Jesus looks at you and loves you.

Questions For Reflection

1. Mark noticed that "Jesus looked at [the wealthy young man] and loved him." When was the last time you considered how God might be looking at you with love?

What would change if you believed that's how He sees you?

2. The woman at the well expected an argument but got a conversation. What arguments with God are keeping you from experiencing His love?

3. Love comes before the challenge to change. Have you been trying to clean yourself up before coming to Jesus? What would it look like to receive His love first?

4. This chapter mentions how Jesus's love isn't "anything-goes love" that leaves people unchanged. How does knowing you're already loved make it easier to receive difficult challenges or truths from God?

5. THE CLEAR TEACHING

The earth is the LORD's, and everything in it. The world and all its people belong to him. (Psalm 24:1)

Remember Nicodemus, the religious expert from the previous chapter? In their late-night conversation, Jesus revealed the clearest statement about God's love: "For God so loved the world that he gave his one and only Son, that whoever believes …" (John 3:16).

Notice the sequence. God loved. Then God gave. Our response comes third—if at all. The Bible is actually pretty explicit about this. God's love isn't a response to our "goodness" or a reward for right belief. It comes first. Not entirely convinced?

Let's examine a few scriptures that teach this concept.

While We Were Still

The Apostle Paul—who experienced God's love while campaigning against it[20]—spelled out the right order with remarkable clarity:

> For while we were still weak, at the right time Christ died for the ungodly. For one will scarcely die for a righteous person—though perhaps for a good person one would dare even to die—but God shows his love for us in that while we were still sinners, Christ died for us. (Romans 5:6-8, ESV)

Let's sit with that phrase: "while we were still…" Still weak. Still ungodly. Still sinners.

It's similar to a line in Jesus's story about the Prodigal Son (Luke 15:14-32). "While he was still a long way off, his father saw him and was filled with compassion for him; he ran to his son, threw his arms around him and kissed him" (Luke 15:20).

"While he was still." See the similarity?

Take note, there's no subtlety here. We weren't good people who needed assistance. We were drowning people who needed a lifeline—and that's when God showed up!

"While we were still."

Think about it. Every other religious system in the world operates on some version of: "Get better, then God will love you. Pray the right prayers. Clean up your act. Then you'll earn divine love."

But True God flips the script. He demonstrates His love. While we were still.

Not Because–But Because

Paul couldn't seem to stop himself from teaching on the theme of "while we were still." Sometimes it had the cadence of: *not because–but because.*

Writing to his apprentice Titus, Paul first painted a stark picture of their former lives:

> At one time we too were foolish, disobedient, deceived and enslaved by all kinds of passions and pleasures. We lived in malice and envy, being hated and hating one another. (Titus 3:3)

Then came that familiar cadence:

> But when the kindness and love of God our Savior appeared, he saved us, *not because* of righteous things we had done, *but because* of his mercy... (Titus 3:4-5, emphasis mine)

This rhythm appears again in his letter to the Ephesians:

> As for you, you were dead in your transgressions and sins... Like the rest, we were by nature deserving of wrath. *But because* of his great love for us, God, who is rich in mercy, made us alive with Christ even when we were dead in transgressions—it is by grace you have been saved. (Ephesians 2:1-5, emphasis mine)

Not because isn't explicitly written in this passage, but it's certainly implicit. We were *dead.* Paul mentions it twice. Think about that word "dead." When someone needs resuscitation, they don't earn it. They can't ask for it.

Someone else must take the initiative.

This echoes back to creation itself: "God formed a man from the dust of the ground and breathed into his nostrils the breath of life" (Genesis 2:7). *Not because*–man earned it, demanded it, or was entitled to it–*but because* of God.

In Him We Live, Move, Exist

Besides writing, the Apostle Paul also did a lot of open-air preaching. His travels once took him to Athens, where he noticed a stone altar dedicated to an "Unknown God."

Paul turned that monument into a message—but what strikes me most isn't his creativity in using a found object to craft his message. It's how he started the talk. He didn't lead with a discussion about sin—most of the Athenian audience wouldn't have connected with that concept anyway.

He started with belonging. Here's the transcript:

> Men of Athens, I notice that you are very religious in every way, for as I was walking along I saw your many shrines. And one of your altars had this inscription on it: "To an Unknown God."
>
> This God, whom you worship without knowing, is the one I'm telling you about. He is the God who made the world and everything in it. Since he is Lord of heaven and earth, he doesn't live in man-made temples, and human hands can't serve his needs—for he has no needs. He himself gives life and breath to everything, and he

> satisfies every need.
>
> From one man he created all the nations throughout the whole earth. He decided beforehand when they should rise and fall, and he determined their boundaries. His purpose was for the nations to seek after God and perhaps feel their way toward him and find him —though he is not far from any one of us.
>
> For in him we live and move and exist. As some of your own poets have said, "We are his offspring." And since this is true, we shouldn't think of God as an idol designed by craftsmen from gold or silver or stone. (Acts 17:22–29, NLT)

Did you catch Paul's last point? "For in him we live and move and exist." Not "in Him, religious people live and move." Not "in Him, Christians exist." But rather, "In Him we (all) live and move and exist."

In other words, we're not trying to get into God's circle. We're already in it. You're not trying to get God's attention. You already have it. You exist within God's care right now, whether you know it, like it, or believe it.

King David knew this and wrote: "The earth is the LORD's, and everything in it. The world and all its people belong to him" (Psalm 24:1).

Everything. All people. Belong to Him.

The Clear Teaching

In the previous chapters on belonging, we explored how God's love works.

In Chapter 2, we saw Jesus use the present perfect "I have loved you" to indicate that His love began in the past and continues now.

In Chapter 3, we discovered how He tends to us while we're unconscious on the roadside, caring for us before we're aware of our need.

In Chapter 4, we saw Jesus love the rich young man, the Samaritan woman, and Nicodemus before challenging them to believe—just as He does for us.

This chapter shows that Jesus's actions were not special cases, but are in perfect alignment with the clear teaching of scripture:

> "God ... breathed ... the breath of life." (Genesis 2:7)
> "The earth is the LORD's, and everything in it." (Psalm 24:1)
> "For God so loved the world..." (John 3:16)
> "For in him we live and move and exist." (Acts 17:28)
> "While we were still sinners..." (Romans 5:8)
> "Not because [of us], but because [of him] ..." (Titus 3:5)

The Bible is clear. God's circle of love comes first.

Speaking of circles, there's something about that shape that captures what we've been exploring in these chapters about the Anchor of Belonging.

But that's for our next chapter. Our final exploration of what it means to belong.

Questions For Reflection

1. The phrase "while we were still" appears throughout Scripture—while still sinners, while still a long way off, while still weak. What were you "still" when you first became aware of God's love?

2. "For God so loved the world that he gave..." God loved first, then gave. How does this order challenge your typical view of earning love or approval—from God or others? Where in your life are you still trying to reverse this order?

3. We're saved "not because of righteous things we had done, but because of his mercy." Be honest: What are you still trying to bring to the table to earn God's love? What "righteous things" are you holding on to that you need to release?

4. Paul told the Athenians "in him we live and move and exist." How does this perspective—that we're already in God's circle rather than trying to get in—change how you think about your relationship with God? What would change in your life if you truly believed you already had God's attention?

6. THE SHAPE OF BELONGING

When the hour came, Jesus and his apostles reclined at the table. (Luke 22:14)

In 2008, my wife Patty and I, along with our kids, moved from North Dakota to China. After a few years studying Mandarin in a city in western China, we relocated to southern China.

Shortly after settling into our new home, Nan appeared at our apartment door. This twelve-year-old boy from two floors down announced that his family had invited us to his grandparents' place for dinner.

We asked him several times, "Are you sure? They really invited us?"

It was the Dragon Boat Festival, a major holiday, and we doubted they'd have room for us. Chinese families typically have one, maybe two children. We had four, ages three to twelve. In addition, we had our friend Jeff living with us. Inviting seven Americans for a traditional Chinese dinner seemed unlikely.

When we walked to Nan's grandparents' apartment, it became immediately obvious he had fabricated the invitation (Nan was outgoing and just wanted our families to be friends).

The elderly couple's eyes widened as our small army filed through their door. They clearly weren't expecting us. But something beautiful happened They scrambled to put together a meal, pulled out extra dishes, sent someone to fetch more *zongzi*,[21] and treated us like honored guests rather than the intrusion we were.

The family's last name can mean "delightful" in Mandarin, and they lived up to it. That awkward first dinner launched a friendship that spanned our entire time in southern China. For two years, we shared meals with this delightful family several times a week.

Around their table, something shifted. The father went from polite curiosity about our presence in China to genuine enthusiasm for our faith. By our final meal together, he was praying over the food and asking me to tell him more about this Jesus we followed.

This family taught us something. In their culture, important matters happen around tables. Business deals, family decisions, relationship milestones—all these and more unfold over shared meals.

The table isn't just where you eat; it's where life happens, strangers become family, and hearts open up between the passing of dishes—which likely explains why Jesus made tables a centerpiece of His ministry.

How Jesus Worked

The phrase "The Son of Man came..." appears in only three sentences in the Gospels. Together, those sentences reveal both his mission and his method.[22] The first two tell us *why* Jesus came:

> "The Son of Man came not to be served but *to serve*, and to *give his life* as a ransom for many." (Mark 10:45, emphasis mine)

> "The Son of Man came *to seek and to save the lost*." (Luke 19:10, emphasis mine)

The third explains *how* He went about it:

> "The Son of Man came *eating and drinking*." (Luke 7:34, emphasis mine)

Jesus's mission was clear: to serve, to seek the lost, and to give His life to save them.

His method, however, was unconventional. He spent time at the table! I like how one author put it, "In Luke's Gospel, Jesus is either going to a meal, at a meal, or coming from a meal."[23]

The Pharisees criticized Him, calling Him a glutton and a drunk, a friend of tax collectors and sinners. They meant it as an insult, but Jesus seemed to take it as a compliment.

The Ordinary Reminder

In 2019, our family prepared to leave China and return to the States to plant a church in Boulder, Colorado. In anticipation of the move, I searched for souvenirs. I don't like the typical tourist trinkets—I prefer unconventional reminders of daily life. My favorite find? A simple wire bike basket. It sits on my desk now as my inbox, but every time I see it, I remember the ordinary rhythms of Chinese life: biking to the office, navigating crowds, carrying groceries home. Not the extraordinary moments, but the everyday stuff of our years there.

This got me thinking about Jesus's departure gift to His disciples. He was about to leave—heading to the cross—and wanted to give them something to remember Him by. As a carpenter, He could have carved beautiful wooden crosses for them to wear. "Wear these in remembrance of me." (Nothing wrong with wearing crosses, of course).

But Jesus didn't choose a religious symbol. Instead—like my bike basket reminder—He chose something His followers would encounter daily.

He chose the table.

The One Reminder

Luke records:

> When the hour came, Jesus and his apostles reclined at the table ... And he took bread, gave thanks and broke it, and gave it to them, saying, "This is my body given for you; do this in remembrance of me." (Luke 22:14, 19)

Jesus chose the most ordinary act to help us remember

Him: a shared meal. He essentially said, "Remember me every time you sit at a table to eat." Not just during communion at church or religious moments. Every meal. Every table. Every time you pass the bread, pour a drink, or make room for one more person to squeeze in.

The Shape Of Belonging

During our eleven years in China, I noticed how common *round* tables were—particularly in many of the finer restaurants. Once, I sat at one that could seat over twenty people.

Round tables are brilliant because you can make eye contact with everyone—not just the person across from you. No one is stuck at the far end, excluded from conversation.

In this book, a circle (figure 6.1) will represent the Belong Anchor.

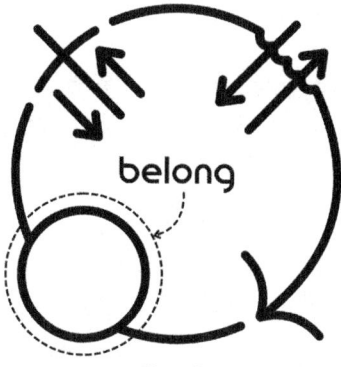

Figure 6.1

Perhaps when you see this circle, you'll think of the shape of our world, calling to mind John 3:16: "For God so loved the world, that he gave his only Son."

Or maybe you'll picture the Lord's beaming face, fully attuned to you, as captured in the Old Testament priestly blessing:

> The Lord bless you and keep you; the Lord make his face shine on you and be gracious to you; the Lord turn his face toward you and give you peace. (Numbers 6:24–26)

Most simply, I hope you'll see the shape of a table where God invites you to dine.[24]

From Table To Trust

Since our arrival in Boulder, we've hosted monthly neighborhood dinners around our table. Our kids once invited Ali, a young man in his twenties, to join us for one of those meals.

Halfway through the evening, Ali asked for everyone's attention. His voice cracked a little as he shared, "Thank you so much for the invitation. I've never felt so loved and included in all my life." Having a meal with our family and neighbors was new to him, and he was profoundly moved.

Ali had been reluctant to talk about God before that night. Religion wasn't his thing; he'd been hurt by it. But something shifted around that table. In the weeks that followed, he went from avoiding spiritual conversations to asking if we could study the Bible together.

The table had done what arguments couldn't. It had opened his heart to consider that maybe this God who sets tables for strangers might be worth listening to.

Will You Listen?

From belonging to considering belief—that's where the Anchored Path leads. You don't have to believe to belong. But if you stay close to Jesus long enough and keep showing up at His table, you'll start to hear Him speak.

Before you turn the page to explore what Jesus has to say, pause and be honest. Are you willing to listen to Him? Has He earned your trust through the circle of His open table?

Belonging is just the beginning. The table is set, you have a place, and you're welcome here. Are you ready to lean in and listen to what He has to say?

Questions For Reflection

1. Recall a time when you felt like an unexpected guest—maybe even an intrusion—but were welcomed anyway. How did that experience of being included when you didn't deserve it affect you?

2. Jesus chose an ordinary table as a place to be remembered. What specific changes could you make to transform your daily meals into more intentional, sacred spaces? How might these changes affect your relationships with others and with Jesus?

3. In this book, a circle represents belonging—a table where everyone can see and be seen. Where in your life have you experienced such belonging? Where are you still seeking it?

4. The chapter ends with this question: "Are you willing

to listen to Him? Has He earned your trust through His welcome, love, and open table?" Consider this question honestly. Where are you in your willingness to hear what Jesus has to say?

ANCHOR TWO: BELIEVE

Jesus was who he said he was or a complete and utter nut case ...You have to make a choice on that. And I believe that Jesus was ... the Son of God.[25] – Bono

I believe in Christianity as I believe that the sun has risen: not only because I see it, but because by it I see everything else.[26] – C.S. Lewis

I have declared to both Jews and Greeks that they must turn to God in repentance and have faith in our Lord Jesus.[27] – Saint Paul

7. FOUR SPIRITUAL TRUTHS

> *We implore you on Christ's behalf: Be reconciled to God. (2 Corinthians 5:20)*

In early 2014, Patty and I moved our family from southern China to northern China where I had the honor of leading an international church. A year or so into our time there, I had a memorable conversation about belief. It started when a young couple—Shan and Soo—came to me for premarital counseling.

Shan was a Chinese law student, and Soo was a Korean woman working for a marketing company. When we first met around our dining room table—the same where my family had eaten a hurried breakfast that morning—I discovered Soo was a Christian, although a nominal believer. Shan, like many Chinese intellectuals, claimed to be an atheist—mixed with a bit of traditional Chinese Buddhism from his grandparents' influence.

Sitting across from them with to-go boba tea between us, I felt my heart sink. I said, "I'm sorry, but we can't proceed with your premarital counseling. Your foundations are too fundamentally different."

My view was based on a passage in one of Paul's letters to the church in Corinth, where he warned young Christians: "Do not be yoked together with unbelievers" (2 Corinthians 6:14). A believer in the God of the Bible navigating life, marriage, and family with a non-believer is a non-starter. Marriage requires a shared foundation for life's biggest decisions—how to handle conflict, raise children, spend money, and find purpose. When one person's north star is Jesus and the other's isn't, you're not just disagreeing about church attendance; you're navigating life with completely different maps.

"Shan," I asked gently, "would you be open to exploring what it means to follow Jesus?"

Shan took a moment to process this. He was clearly in love with Soo and also intelligent, honest, and thoughtful. He wasn't about to say he believed just so I'd proceed with marriage counseling.

"I'd like to believe, but I can't get past the story of creation and how everything came to be. My whole life I've been taught the theory of evolution, so it's hard to accept the idea that a God created everything."

Some people would love to engage in that conversation and prove God is the creator, but I found myself saying, "You know, Shan, let's put that aside for right now. The most important thing that you need to think about is this

—what are you going to do with Jesus?"

After a short pause, I asked him, "Can I share four spiritual truths you need to understand to know what it means to be a Christian?"

Shan nodded and pulled out a small notebook, prepared to analyze and understand.

1. God Loves You And Desires A Relationship With You

"First, Shan, you need to know that God loves you and He desires to have a relationship with you."

Shan's eyebrows rose slightly. This was news to him, as it is to many. People either don't believe in God or, if they do, they see Him as distant and uninterested—especially if they are from a place where religion has been suppressed for decades.

When we explored the Anchor of Belonging earlier in this book, it was to establish this vital truth: You're loved by God, no matter who you are or where you come from. Remember the line from Paul's sermon back in Chapter 5?

> His purpose was for the nations to seek after God and perhaps feel their way toward him and find him—though he is not far from any one of us. For in him we live and move and exist. (Acts 17:27–28, NLT)

Just as I wanted Shan to notice, I want *you* to notice: God's purpose for your life is to reach out to Him. To respond to His invitation. To move from the Anchor of Belonging to the secure Anchor of Believing.

Let's continue my conversation with Shan.

2. Your Sin Separates You From God

"Second," I said to Shan, "Your sin separates you from the relationship God desires to have with you."

"Surely the arm of the Lord is not too short to save," I read from Isaiah, "nor his ear too dull to hear. But your iniquities [sins] have separated you from your God" (Isaiah 59:1-2).

"Shan, do you know what sin is?"

"Yeah, I think so. It's like ... doing something bad? Violating a code?"

Shan's law education and exposure to Buddhism gave him a basic understanding of sin. In fact, Christianity, Judaism, Islam, Hinduism, and Buddhism all share the concept.

"For Christians," I said, "to sin is to break God's Law, which everyone (other than Jesus) has done."

I turned in my Bible to Romans 3:23. "For all have sinned," Shan read, "and fall short of the glory of God."

I saw Shan nodding slowly, his eyes thoughtful rather than defensive. I didn't need to convince him that all people, including himself, have sinned.

My conversation with Shan was focused on the simple truth that we all fall short of God's standards. But for you, the reader, I want to take a moment to unpack what we mean by God's Law more fully. There are three key forms we should understand: the law of Moses, the law of Jesus, and the law on our heart.

The Law Of Moses

The Law of God usually refers to the Law of Moses—the Ten Commandments.[28] We saw how Jesus used these commandments in His interaction with the rich young man in Mark 10. When the young man asked, "What must I do to inherit eternal life?" (Mark 10:17), Jesus began by pointing him to the Law of Moses.

> "You know the commandments: 'You shall not murder, you shall not commit adultery, you shall not steal, you shall not give false testimony, you shall not defraud, honor your father and mother.'"
>
> "Teacher," he declared, "all these I have kept since I was a boy." (Mark 10:19–20)

But had he really? For this young man, the Law, which God intended to create a loving, civil society in connection with Him, had become just something to memorize—not to truly live out. The truth is: he couldn't live them out. Neither can anyone.

The Law Of Jesus

The Law of God can also refer to something Jesus said. He was once asked, "Which is the greatest commandment?" (Matthew 22:36).

Jesus replied:

> "'Love the Lord your God with all your heart and with all your soul and with all your mind.' This is the first and greatest commandment. And the second is like it: 'Love your neighbor as yourself.' All the Law and the Prophets hang on these two commandments." (Matthew 22:37–40)

In that conversation, Jesus didn't change the Law. He summarized it: Love God,[29] love people.[30]

And it's these Ten-Summarized-in-Two Laws that Jesus dropped on the young man (after being interrupted by him) in Mark 10:

> "One thing you lack," he said. "Go, sell everything you have and give to the poor, and you will have treasure in heaven. Then come, follow me." At this the man's face fell. He went away sad, because he had great wealth. (Mark 10:21–22)

In Jesus's one short comment, the young man became aware of his sin. He was breaking the most important Law of Jesus—"Love the Lord your God with all your heart, soul, and mind"—because he couldn't bring himself to follow God (even as God stood there in the person of Jesus). He was also breaking the second most important Law of Jesus—"love your neighbor as yourself"—because he couldn't bring himself to care for his fellow man.

The young man was still loved, but he was outed as a selfish lawbreaker, and now he knew it. And he willfully chose continued separation from God rather than fellowship—a choice with consequences that extend beyond this life into eternity.

The Law On Our Heart

The Law of God can also refer to what is "written on [our] hearts". In his letter to the Romans, Paul wrote:

> Indeed, when Gentiles, who do not have the law, do by nature things required by the law [either the Law of Moses or Jesus's summary] they are a law for themselves, even though they do not have the law. They show that the requirements of the law are written on their hearts... (Romans 2:14–15)

In psychology, this internal moral compass is called our conscience—from *con* (with) and *science* (knowledge). It's our built-in awareness of right and wrong.

How do we know when we're violating this heart-written law? We lose our peace. As Paul wrote to the Colossians, "Let the peace that comes from Christ rule in your hearts" (Colossians 3:15, NLT). When that peace isn't ruling, neither is Christ—and we end up violating His Law.

We're still loved by God—but we're unreconciled to God.[31]

Let's return to my conversation with Shan. I drew a simple diagram for him: a broken line on a piece of paper from one of our kids' notebooks (figure 7.1).

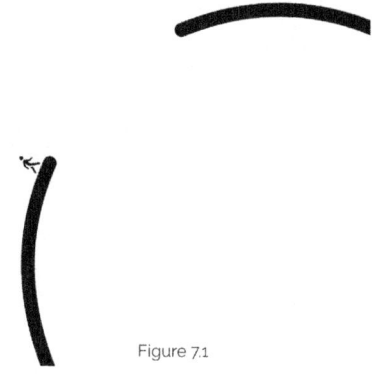

Figure 7.1

On the left, I sketched a stick figure of a person. "Because of our sin, we're *here*, eternally separated from God," I explained. Then I pointed at the right side. "While God wants us to be in relationship with Him *here* ... but ... this distance is too great for us to cross on our own."

"What do we do?" Shan asked.

"Nothing. We can't do a thing about it—but God did."

3. Jesus Paid The Price For Your Sin

I filled in the gap of the line with a cross (figure 7.2).

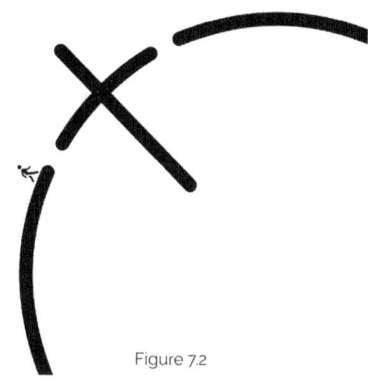

Figure 7.2

"This is the good news, Shan. Jesus paid the price for your sins on the cross; he was punished in your place. You and I *should* have been crucified for our sins, but Jesus said, 'I will take the punishment for them.'"

I opened my Bible to Romans 5:6-8 and read, "'When we were still powerless'—which means we couldn't cross the divide on our own," I explained, "'Christ died for the ungodly. Very rarely will anyone die for a righteous person, though for a good person someone might possibly dare to die. But God demonstrates his own love for us in this: While we were still sinners, Christ died for us.'"

I asked, "Ready for the fourth spiritual truth?"

"Yes." Shan leaned in.

4. You Have A Choice

"You have a choice. That's the final truth, Shan."

I turned in my Bible and read John 3:16:[32] "For God so loved the world that he gave his one and only Son, that whoever believes in him shall not perish but have eternal life."

"Do you see that, Shan? 'Whoever believes'—meaning we all have a choice. Will you trust in Jesus and the price He paid? Will you cross from where you are to where God desires you to be? Will you believe?"

I paused, letting the question settle in our dining room. Outside, traffic hummed its constant song, but inside, everything felt still.

Shan isn't the only one to have wrestled with this question. It's a question for all of us. Will *you* believe in Jesus? Will you trust in the sacrifice He made for you? Will you receive God's forgiveness and be reconciled to Him?

It's important to note: I'm not asking you to be loved. God already loves you and there's nothing you can do about it. The choice is whether you'll love Him back. Put Him first. Trust Him with your life.

Eternity hangs in the balance, but I didn't want Shan—and I don't want you—to make a quick decision.

"You don't have to tell me now," I said to Shan. "As you leave tonight, think about this. But within three days, please get back to me. Send a text and tell me what you decide."

The Longest Three Days

Three days passed without a text from Shan. I found myself checking my phone constantly. Each morning, I prayed at that dining room table, "Lord, work in Shan's heart. Help him see your love." By the evening of the third day, I was discouraged and thought, "I guess he's made his decision."

That night, I wrestled with whether I should have handled things differently. Should I have addressed his creation question first? Had I pushed too hard? Not hard enough?

But on the fourth day, my phone buzzed. The text was simple: "Sorry this is late, but I want to believe in Jesus.

Can we meet again soon?"

My anxious waiting gave way to gratitude. He hadn't just made a decision—he was ready to act on it.

We met at a KFC near my apartment. The irony wasn't lost on me—discussing eternal matters amid the smell of fried chicken and the chatter of college students. But somehow, the ordinary setting made the moment more sacred.

I reminded Shan of the four spiritual truths we discussed earlier in the week at my home.

"Shan, are you ready to believe in Jesus and walk across the gap?"

His voice was steady and certain. "I am."

"All right, here's what I'd like you to do. I'd like you to pray—which means I want you to talk to God—and just let Him know what's on your heart."

I instructed him to include two vital ingredients in his prayer: repentance and faith. In other words, I encouraged him to let God know he was sorry for his sin and ready to trust in Jesus for forgiveness.

In the noisy KFC, with pop music blaring and cash registers dinging, Shan bowed his head and prayed, repenting of his sin and placing his faith in Jesus.

Repentance And Faith

In my talk with Shan about believing in Jesus, I stressed two essentials: repentance and faith. These are foundational for belief, and are the next focus in this book.

But before we continue, let's pause to reflect. The four spiritual truths I shared with Shan aren't just relevant to his story—they're relevant to yours too. The same God who pursued Shan at my dining room table is pursuing you right now, wherever you're reading this.

The question remains: Will you choose to believe in Jesus?

Questions For Reflection

1. Like Shan, many people have intellectual or emotional barriers to belief. What questions or doubts make it difficult for you to fully trust Jesus? How might temporarily setting aside these secondary issues help you focus on the central question: "What will you do with Jesus?"

2. Of the three forms of God's Law discussed (Moses, Jesus, and Heart), which most clearly reveals areas where you've fallen short? Describe a time when you experienced that internal loss of peace that signals a violation of God's law.

3. Think back to the diagram I drew for Shan showing the gap sin creates between us and God, with the cross as the bridge. If you were to draw your spiritual journey, where would you place yourself right now—still on the left side, standing at the cross, or somewhere on the right? What's keeping you from moving forward?

4. I gave Shan three days to think before deciding. If someone gave you the same timeline today, what would you need to process or resolve before responding?

8. MORE THAN SORRY

> *Jesus began to preach, "Repent, for the kingdom of heaven has come near." (Matthew 4:17)*

What does it mean to believe in Jesus? Is it just mental agreement with certain facts? Or adhering to a set of rules?

For many, belief has been reduced to checking a doctrinal box or following a behavioral checklist. But biblical belief is far more transformational—it's a complete reorientation of our lives.

As Shan discovered in that KFC, biblical belief has two essential ingredients: repentance and faith. Many sermons of the early church emphasized this two-part response.

Jesus preached, "The kingdom of God has come near. Repent and believe the good news!" (Mark 1:15).

8. MORE THAN SORRY

Paul preached, "Turn to God in repentance and have faith in our Lord Jesus" (Acts 20:21).

Peter preached, "Repent, then, and turn to God, so that your sins may be wiped out, that times of refreshing may come from the Lord" (Acts 3:19).

Notice the pattern? Repentance and faith. Turn and trust. Think of them as inhale and exhale—life depends on doing both.

However, many people try to skip one or the other. Some want faith without repentance ("I'll trust Jesus but keep living my way"). Others attempt repentance without faith ("I'll try to be better on my own and earn my way"). Neither approach gives life.

Let's examine what these two elements mean. In the next chapter, we'll explore the essence of faith. In this chapter, we'll focus our thoughts on repentance.

To start, picture the broken line from chapter 7 with the stick figure on the left, a relationship with God on the right, and the cross bridging the gap (figure 7.2). Now, in the image below, notice the downward "REPENT" arrow to the left of the cross (figure 8.1).

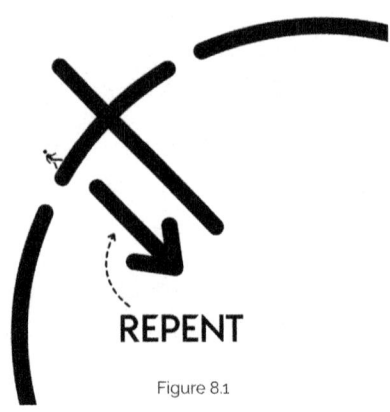

Figure 8.1

To understand this image, we have to ask, what does it mean to repent?

Many of us carry baggage around this word. For some, repentance means groveling in shame, beating ourselves up until God decides we've suffered enough. For others, it's a quick "my bad, God" before moving on unchanged. Still others see it as an outdated concept, something fire-and-brimstone preachers ungraciously shout about.

Biblical repentance is none of these things. It's actually a complete whole-bodied reorientation—a literal "turning around" of our hearts and lives.

I'd like to suggest that repentance involves six movements, represented by the letters of REPENT.

Recognize Your Sin

In the last chapter, we looked at the Law of God, which included the Law of Moses, Jesus, and Our Heart. The point was to help us see that we are all sinners. This is a primary purpose of the Law; it shows how short we fall of God's standard.[33]

However, the Law isn't the only way to be confronted with our sin. Sometimes, we just need a fresh vision of God's perfection and power. As we do, we understand how imperfect and powerless we are.

Take Simon Peter as an example. His first encounter with Jesus was rather abrupt. Jesus co-opted his boat as a podium and began to preach to the crowd. Let's pick up the story as Jesus concludes His sermon:

> When [Jesus] had finished speaking, he said to Simon [Peter], "Put out into deep water, and let down the nets for a catch."
>
> Simon answered, "Master, we've worked hard all night and haven't caught anything. But because you say so, I will let down the nets."
>
> When they had done so, they caught such a large number of fish that their nets began to break. So they signaled their partners in the other boat to come and help them, and they came and filled both boats so full that they began to sink.
>
> When Simon Peter saw this, he fell at Jesus' knees and said, "Go away from me, Lord; I am a sinful man!" (Luke 5:4–8)

Notice: Jesus's preaching didn't bring Simon to his knees —the miracle did. Suddenly he saw himself clearly: "Go away from me, Lord; I am a sinful man!" (Luke 5:8). In that moment of divine intervention, Simon Peter recognized the gap between God and man—between Jesus and himself.

Recognizing our sin isn't about comparing ourselves with

other people and their imperfections. It's about seeing ourselves in light of God and His perfection—perfect in glory, majesty, and power.

When Isaiah witnessed God's glory, he said, "Woe to me! I am ruined! I am a man of unclean lips!" (Isaiah 6:5).

When Job encountered God's majesty, he said, "I despise myself and repent in dust and ashes" (Job 42:6).

When Paul experienced God's power, he fell to the ground and cried, "What shall I do, Lord?" (Acts 22:10).

Recognizing our sin is using our *heads* to make an honest self-assessment. It's like walking into a room you assumed was clean, turning on the lights, and acknowledging the filth and chaos you've been living with.

Whether by looking at the Law of God or the power and perfection of His beauty—take a moment to let the light of His Love reveal the reality of your sin.

Experience Godly Sorrow

After raising four kids, Patty and I learned to recognize different types of tears.

Some were angry tears: "I'd have gotten away with it if I'd covered my tracks better!"

Others were performance tears—a calculated display when caught red-handed, hoping the waterworks might soften the consequences.

Then there were the truly sorrowful tears. Not regret over getting caught, but genuine remorse in their *hearts* over causing pain. This kind of sorrow cuts deeper—it's feeling the weight of harm we've caused God, ourselves, and others.

King David experienced this godly sorrow. He committed crimes that would earn the rest of us a lifetime sentence: he stole a man's wife and had the man murdered (2 Samuel 11). In Psalm 51, he expressed his remorse:

> Have mercy on me, O God, according to your unfailing love; according to your great compassion blot out my transgressions. Wash away all my iniquity and cleanse me from my sin. For I know my transgressions, and my sin is always before me. Against you, you only, have I sinned and done what is evil in your sight; so you are right in your verdict and justified when you judge. (Psalm 51:1-4)

David wasn't just ashamed of getting caught or sad that his life was about to fall apart.[34] His heart was broken over the reality of what he'd done—especially how it had damaged his relationship with God:

"Against you, you only, have I sinned" (Psalm 51:4).

Wait—only against God? What about the woman he stole, or the husband he had killed?

David understood something profound: all sin is ultimately against God. When we lie to people, we sin against God. When we view online porn, we sin against God. When we harbor bitterness and unforgiveness, we sin against God. Sadly, other people are often serious collateral damage—but sin is first and foremost a breach in our relationship with our Creator.

Paul distinguishes between this "godly" sorrow and "worldly" sorrow. He says, "Godly sorrow brings repentance that leads to salvation and leaves no regret, but worldly sorrow brings death" (2 Corinthians 7:10).

Worldly sorrow is self-focused. It's like my kids' angry tears when caught. It's about our loss, our reputation, and our discomfort. It turns us inward toward self-pity.

Godly sorrow—true remorse—is other-focused. Our heart grieves the pain we've caused God and others. This sorrow doesn't paralyze us; it propels us toward change.

The difference? Worldly sorrow says, "I can't believe I got caught." Godly sorrow says, "I can't believe the pain I've inflicted." One leads to death, the other to life.

Before moving forward, take a moment. Has your *heart* moved beyond regret to genuine godly sorrow? Not just sorry for the sin, but broken over the pain it caused?

Pray For Forgiveness

When our kids were young, we taught them that "sorry" wasn't sufficient when they hurt someone.

Our rationale: saying "sorry" keeps you in control. You chose to hurt someone, and now you expect them to snap back to normal because you apologized. That's not how forgiveness works. A mere "sorry" assumes a reset without repair.

We required them to vocalize at least two parts:[35] "I'm sorry ... will you *forgive* me?"

The question "Will you forgive me?" was essential. It

gave the offended party (usually a sibling) the power to grant forgiveness. It taught the offending party that forgiveness is not something we demand—it's something we ask and pray for.

David modeled this prayer in the Psalm we just read: "Have mercy on me, O God" (Psalm 51:1).

Jesus told a parable about a tax collector who prayed a similar prayer:

> Two men went up to the temple to pray, one a Pharisee and the other a tax collector.
>
> The Pharisee stood by himself and prayed: "God, I thank you that I am not like other people—robbers, evildoers, adulterers—or even like this tax collector. I fast twice a week and give a tenth of all I get."
>
> But the tax collector stood at a distance. He would not even look up to heaven, but beat his breast and said, "God, have mercy on me, a sinner."
>
> I tell you that this man, rather than the other, went home justified [forgiven] before God. For all those who exalt themselves will be humbled, and those who humble themselves will be exalted. (Luke 18:10–14)

The tax collector's prayer is remarkable. No excuses. No comparisons. No bargaining. Just a seven-word plea from his *mouth:* "God, have mercy on me, a sinner" (Luke 18:13). This is the posture of repentance: not informing God of our apology, but praying for His forgiveness.

Notice how the Pharisee's prayer was about what he'd done right, while the tax collector's was about what only God could make right. Who went home forgiven? Not the religious expert—but the man who begged for mercy. This man understood that forgiveness isn't something we demand; it's something we ask for. And God, "rich in mercy" (Ephesians 2:4), loves to answer that prayer.

Take a moment. Is your pride still trying to control the situation with God, or is your heart moved to open your *mouth* and genuinely pray: "I'm sorry, Lord ... will you forgive me?"

Spoiler alert: He will.[36]

Embrace Making Amends

Years ago on a camping trip, my nephew accidentally dropped my son Noah's pocketknife into a deep creek pool. Despite everyone's efforts, it was lost. Noah's cousin apologized. "I'm sorry, Noah ... will you forgive me?"

But then my brother-in-law did something more. He took his son to a local Walmart to buy Noah a replacement pocketknife. I've always felt odd allowing Noah to accept that gift of restitution because our culture has largely abandoned the practice of making amends.

Making amends means doing what you can to tangibly correct a mistake. It's asking—then acting—on the question, "What can I do to make this right?" Making amends is an indicator of real repentance. Paul saw it as evidence of the Corinthians' godly sorrow.

The Corinthian church had hurt Paul deeply—tolerating

false teachers, questioning his authority, and allowing divisive people to turn them against him. But after Paul confronted them in a painful letter, they experienced genuine remorse and wanted to make things right. In response, Paul wrote:

> See what this godly sorrow has produced in you: what earnestness, what eagerness to clear yourselves, what indignation, what alarm, what longing, what concern, what readiness to see justice done. (2 Corinthians 7:11)

Do you hear it? The Corinthians were essentially asking, "We made a mistake, how can we fix it? How can we restore and provide restitution? How can we actively make amends?"

When Zacchaeus encountered Jesus, he instinctively knew that making amends was part of repentance. Zacchaeus was a chief tax collector—basically a traitor to his own people who got rich by overcharging his fellow Jews and skimming off the top. Watch what happens when he meets Jesus:

> But Zacchaeus stood up and said to the Lord, "Look, Lord! Here and now I give half of my possessions to the poor, and if I have cheated anybody out of anything, I will pay back four times the amount."
>
> Jesus said to him, "Today salvation has come to this house, because this man, too, is a son of Abraham. For the Son of Man came to seek and to save the lost." (Luke 19:8–10)

Jesus didn't demand he make amends. Zacchaeus

volunteered it. It was a natural result of genuine repentance and forgiveness.

When we embrace making amends, we begin the uncomfortable process of clearing away the rubble of our old life to build something new. It won't be perfect—I'm sure Zacchaeus couldn't undo every wrong. But where possible, we make things right.

Sometimes this means having difficult conversations. Sometimes it means changing habits or environments. It almost always means doing the hard thing.

Think of it this way: if repentance starts in our *mind* as we recognize our sin, moves to our *heart* as we experience sorrow, and comes out of our *mouth* as we pray for forgiveness, then it should show up in our *hands* as we make amends in tangible ways.

Pause and reflect, "Where and with whom do I need to embrace making amends?"

Nurture New Fruit

Making amends addresses what's behind us, clearing away the debris of past mistakes. But like a farmer who doesn't stop with a cleared field, true repentance moves beyond cleanup to cultivation. God calls us to nurture new life.

Jesus's cousin John (known as John the Baptist) was a prophet in the most iconic sense—camel hair clothing, leather belt, untrimmed beard—and his message was as confrontational as his looks: "Repent, for the kingdom of heaven has come near" (Matthew 3:2).

8. MORE THAN SORRY

For John, repentance meant more than recognizing sin, experiencing sorrow, praying for forgiveness, or making amends. He was just as concerned with our life going forward. "Produce fruit in keeping with repentance," he preached. "The ax is already at the root of the trees, and every tree that does not produce good fruit will be cut down and thrown into the fire" (Matthew 3:8,10).

Jesus's brother James preached the same message:

> What good is it, my brothers and sisters, if someone claims to have faith but has no deeds? Can such faith save them? Suppose a brother or a sister is without clothes and daily food. If one of you says to them, "Go in peace; keep warm and well fed," but does nothing about their physical needs, what good is it? In the same way, faith by itself, if it is not accompanied by action, is dead. (James 2:14–17)

The message is clear: real repentance results in real change. Our *feet* take steps in a new direction. We begin to produce new fruit—new mindsets and behaviors that evidence the change.

The fruit might be small at first—newfound patience with your coworkers, unexpected generosity toward a difficult neighbor, surprising peace in traffic. But as we walk with Jesus, the fruit becomes evident. Love, joy, peace, patience, kindness, goodness, faithfulness, gentleness, and self-control begin to characterize our lives (Galatians 5:22).

Pause. Can you sense the Holy Spirit moving you to nurture new fruit? Where and how will you start?

Thank God

Thomas Watson was a pastor in London during the 1600s—a time when Christians were rediscovering God's grace after years of cold legalism. He wrote practical, devotional works, emphasizing God's mercy over human effort.

In his nearly 400-year-old book *The Doctrine of Repentance*, he writes: "Repentance is a grace of God's Spirit whereby a sinner is inwardly humbled and visibly reformed."[37]

"A *grace* of God's Spirit," says Watson. Paul confirms this when he writes, "God's kindness is intended to lead you to repentance" (Romans 2:4). In other words, repentance is a *gift* from God.

How do we respond to a gift? We simply say "thank you."

> Like Peter, we thank God for helping our minds recognize our sin.
>
> Like David, we thank God that He gave us hearts to experience godly sorrow.
>
> Like the tax collector, we thank God for hearing our prayers for forgiveness.
>
> Like Zacchaeus, we thank God for moving our hands to make amends.
>
> Like John's hearers, we thank God for feet that walk in a new direction and lives that produce new fruit.

Like Paul, we thank God for His kindness that led us to repent.

Remember the downward arrow—the one to the left of the cross (figure 8.1)? That's what we've just walked through. The humbling, turning, letting go as we cross the bridge Jesus provides.

The whole-bodied movement of REPENT (figure 8.2) has brought us lower, not into shame, but into grace. We've descended from pride into gratitude, from self-sufficiency into God-dependence.

This is repentance—but it's only half of belief. Biblical belief has two arrows aligned with the cross: repentance and faith.

We'll discuss faith in the next chapter, but for now, take a moment to simply thank God for the gift of repentance. What specific aspects of your repentance journey can you thank Him for?

A Prayer Of Repentance

If the following words echo your heart, please use them as a prayer of repentance, or let them inspire your own prayer:

> *Lord, like Peter, I recognize that I am a sinner. When I see Your glory, majesty, and power, my first instinct is to say, "Go away from me, Lord, I am a sinful person!" (Luke 5:8). But I know You draw close to the brokenhearted and save those who are crushed in spirit (Psalm 34:18).*

I feel genuine sorrow—not just worldly regret—but true godly sorrow for the pain my sin has caused You and others (2 Corinthians 7:10). Against You only have I ultimately sinned (Psalm 51:4).

So, I pray like the tax collector: "God, have mercy on me, a sinner" (Luke 18:13). I'm not just telling You I'm sorry—I'm asking, will You forgive me?

Like Zacchaeus, show me where I need to make amends (Luke 19:8). Give me courage to have hard conversations and make things right where I can (2 Corinthians 7:11). Help me nurture new fruit in keeping with repentance—patience, kindness, love—the evidence of a changed life (Matthew 3:8, Galatians 5:22-23).

And Lord, thank You. Thank You that repentance itself is Your gift to me. Thank You for Your kindness that leads me to turn around. Thank You that I don't have to manufacture this on my own—You make it possible (Romans 2:4).

In Jesus's name, Amen.[38]

Questions For Reflection

1. When have you experienced a "Peter moment"—a time when witnessing God's power, holiness, or glory suddenly made you aware of your own sinfulness? How was that different from simply comparing yourself to other people or religious standards?

2. Think about a specific area where you've recently struggled. Describe the difference between worldly sorrow (being sorry you got caught, upset about

consequences) and godly sorrow (grief over pain caused). Where are you in that journey from worldly sorrow to godly sorrow?

3. As you consider the six movements of REPENT, which one is most difficult for you personally: recognizing your sin, experiencing godly sorrow, praying for mercy, embracing making amends, nurturing new fruit, or thanking God? What makes that particular step challenging?

4. Making amends can feel uncomfortable or even impossible. Who do you need to have a hard conversation with, and what would you need to say or do to begin clearing away the rubble of past hurt?

5. The Holy Spirit may be prompting you about new fruit He wants to develop in your life. What specific change is He calling you toward, and what's one practical step you could take this week to begin nurturing that fruit?

6. How does understanding repentance as God's gift (something He enables through His kindness) rather than your religious duty (something you must manufacture) change your attitude toward both past failures and ongoing struggles?

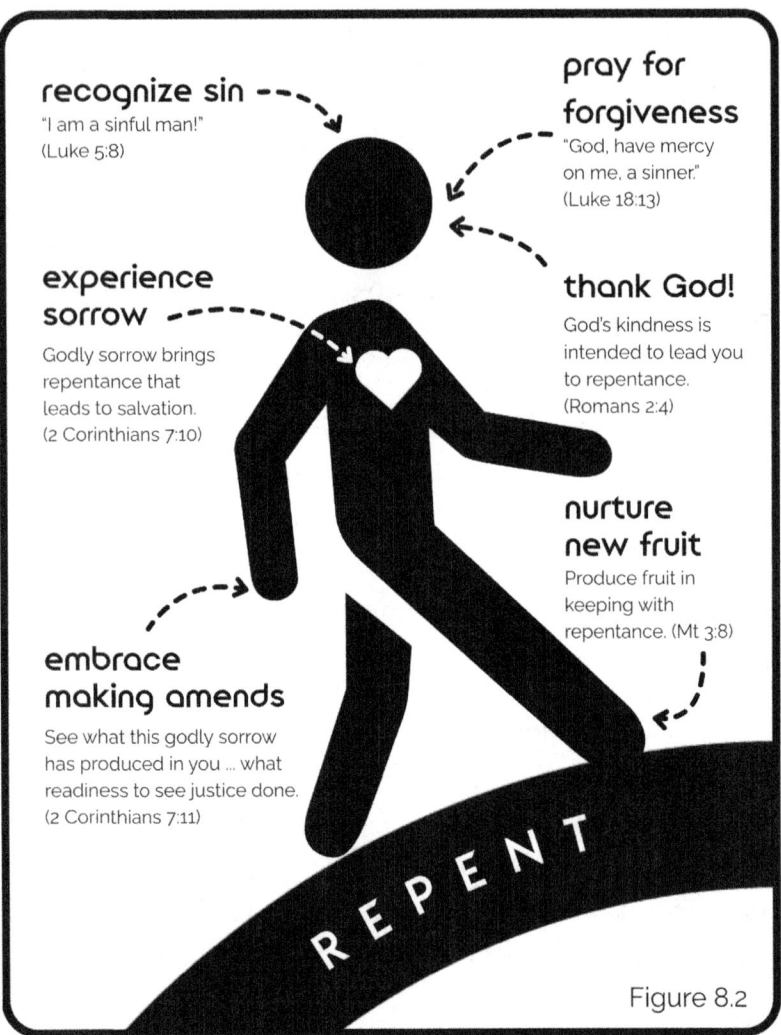

Figure 8.2

9. THE ESSENCE OF FAITH

Now faith is confidence in what we hope for and assurance about what we do not see. This is what the ancients were commended for. (Hebrews 11:1–2)

During our time in China, I got into roasting coffee—mostly out of necessity. Finding a decent cup of coffee in a tea culture proved challenging enough that I decided to take matters into my own hands.

Before I could enjoy a cup, my green beans had to undergo a crucial transformation. Without dedicated equipment, I'd dump them into a cast iron pan on our gas stove. Then, I'd stir constantly with a whisk as they crackled and popped, slowly darkening from jade to medium-brown.

Despite the roasting, the whole beans still wouldn't make drinkable coffee. They had to be ground—broken open to expose what the fire had created. Then, when hot water poured over the crushed grounds, something remarkable happened. The water lifted out the oils and essences, carrying the fragrance upward in steam while creating something new: a wonderful cup of fresh morning coffee.

As we believe in Jesus and walk the gap by way of His cross, we undergo a similar process. Remember the down-pointing repentance arrow on the left of the cross (figure 8.1)? Good news: there's also an up-pointing faith arrow on the right (figure 9.1).

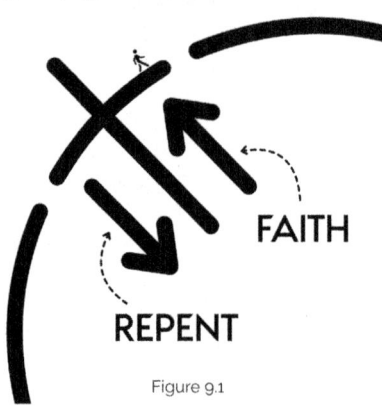

Figure 9.1

The downward arrow of repentance is like grinding roasted beans. You may have felt that brokenness during the movements of REPENT in the previous chapter. This crushing isn't pleasant, but it prepares us for what comes next.

The upward arrow of faith is like hot water lifting the fragrance from broken coffee grounds. God's Spirit pours over our repentant hearts, enables faith, and transforms us into something new. As Jesus says, we're "born again."[39]

But what does it mean to have faith? We often narrow this word, reducing it to a hopeful wish or mental agreement. Biblical faith is richer, fuller, and more robust. Its essence can be described with the five letters of FAITH.

Factual

I was born in 1972, and I'm writing in 2025. Ever wonder why our years have those numbers? Why was my birth year called "1972," and why is the current year called "2025"?

It's because the vast majority of our world marks the literal calendar years since the birth of Jesus Christ—a very real, flesh-and-blood person born 2,025 years ago.

Consider this: Jesus splits the global timeline in two. We mark the years before His birth and after His birth. Jesus isn't merely an idea, spiritual experience, or religious opinion. His birth, death, and resurrection are historical events—facts supported by evidence, not just religious claims.[40]

I'm making this point because the earliest Jesus followers strove to make the same point. John wrote a letter to the early church, using sensory detail to illustrate how real Jesus was:

> That which was from the beginning, which we have heard, which we have seen with our eyes, which we have looked at and our hands have touched—this we proclaim concerning the Word of life. The life appeared; we have seen it and testify to it, and we proclaim to you the eternal life, which was with the Father and has appeared to us. We proclaim to you what we have seen and heard... (1 John 1:1–3)

Paul wrote to early believers, emphasizing that many witnesses—not just a handful—saw the risen Jesus:

> For what I received I passed on to you as of first importance: that Christ died for our sins according to the Scriptures, that he was buried, that he was raised on the third day according to the Scriptures, and that he appeared to Cephas, and then to the Twelve. After that, he appeared to more than five hundred of the brothers and sisters at the same time... (1 Corinthians 15:3-6)

Peter made the same emphatic point about eyewitness testimony:

> For we did not follow cleverly devised stories when we told you about the coming of our Lord Jesus Christ in power, but we were eyewitnesses of his majesty. (2 Peter 1:16)

Here's the point: faith isn't built on a feeling or idea. It's built on what's actually true. This is where we start. Our culture tells us that personal, subjective experience is the ultimate authority. But Christian faith starts by mentally acknowledging the objective fact that Jesus really did exist.[41]

The writer of Hebrews says:

> And without faith it is impossible to please God, because anyone who comes to him must believe that he exists and that he rewards those who earnestly seek him. (Hebrews 11:6)

But using our *heads* to acknowledge that Jesus existed, died, and rose again is just the beginning of faith.

Actual

The essence of biblical faith goes beyond facts—it's something that is actually true of *us*. We don't just believe Jesus existed in our heads. Our *hearts* place faith in Him, too.

Faith means hearing Jesus's question to His disciples—and answering like Peter. Let's look at that conversation:

> [Jesus] asked his disciples, "Who do people say the Son of Man is?"
>
> They replied, "Some say John the Baptist; others say Elijah; and still others, Jeremiah or one of the prophets."
>
> "But what about you?" he asked. "Who do you say I am?"
>
> Simon Peter answered, "You are the Messiah, the Son of the living God." (Matthew 16:13–16)

C.S. Lewis famously framed this choice in *Mere Christianity*:

> I am trying here to prevent anyone saying the really foolish thing that people often say about Him: I'm ready to accept Jesus as a great moral teacher, but I don't accept his claim to be God.
>
> That is the one thing we must not say. A man who was merely a man and said the sort of things Jesus said would not be a great moral teacher. He would either be a lunatic—on the level with the man who says he is a poached egg

—or else he would be the Devil of Hell.

You must make your choice. Either this man was, and is, the Son of God, or else a madman or something worse. You can shut him up for a fool, you can spit at him and kill him as a demon or you can fall at his feet and call him Lord and God, but let us not come with any patronizing nonsense about his being a great human teacher. He has not left that open to us. He did not intend to...

Now it seems to me obvious that He was neither a lunatic nor a fiend: and consequently, however strange or terrifying or unlikely it may seem, I have to accept the view that He was and is God.[42]

I remember talking to my friend and fellow musician Mike, who was struggling with taking this step from factual faith to actual faith. In his mind, the issue wasn't whether or not Jesus had surrendered His life for Mike. It was whether or not Mike was willing to surrender his life to Jesus. Would he take the step from believing in his head to believing with his *heart*?

This wasn't a small step for Mike. It's not a small step for anyone! But, I'm happy to report that after months of playing guitar together and talking about faith, Mike (in his words) went "all in" and surrendered—he placed his faith in Jesus.

How about you? Who do you say Jesus is? Will you go beyond believing *that* Jesus existed to believing *in* the Jesus who exists? Will your faith shift from objective information *about* Him to subjective confidence *in* Him?[43] Will you allow faith to drop from your head to your heart, and let the factual become actual?

If You Declare

If you've made the faith journey like Mike did, then the next place your faith shows up should be quite natural: your *mouth*.

Thomas was one of Jesus's 12 disciples. Like the rest, his journey of faith started with his head: He knew and believed Jesus existed. He had walked and talked with Jesus for three years. Jesus wasn't a product of his imagination; He was real.

Thomas was absent when the risen Jesus first appeared to the other disciples. Upon hearing the news of the resurrection and the empty tomb, Thomas initially doubted: "Unless I see the nail marks in his hands and put my finger where the nails were, and put my hand into his side, I will not believe" (John 20:25).

When they finally met a week later, Jesus said to Thomas, "Put your finger here; see my hands. Reach out your hand and put it into my side. Stop doubting and believe" (John 20:27).

In that singular moment, Thomas's faith moved from his head to his heart—and then quite spontaneously to his *mouth*, as he said to Jesus, "My Lord and my God!" (John 20:28).

This is the journey each of us must take. We begin by acknowledging in our *minds* that Jesus is a fact. He was and is real. We then embrace this truth in our *hearts*—making it personal and actual. We believe Jesus lived, still lives, and is everything the Bible says He is. Finally, we declare this faith with our *mouths*. Paul wrote to the Romans:

> If you declare with your mouth, "Jesus is Lord," and believe in your heart that God raised him from the dead, you will be saved. For it is with your heart that you believe and are justified, and it is with your mouth that you profess your faith and are saved. (Romans 10:9–10)

"For the mouth speaks what the heart is full of," Jesus said (Matthew 12:34). That's why declaring faith is natural and essential. It shows what's actually true in your heart. If your mind and heart have put their faith in Jesus, your mouth will declare it.

Together With

The essence of faith doesn't end with your mouth. The last thing the world needs is another person declaring "Jesus is Lord" with their lips while their life tells a different story. Faith must also show up in your *hands*—in what you actually do.

James, Jesus's brother, didn't mince words:

> Show me your faith without deeds, and I will show you my faith by my deeds. You believe that there is one God. Good! Even the demons believe that—and shudder.
>
> You foolish person, do you want evidence that

faith without deeds is useless? Was not our father Abraham considered righteous for what he did when he offered his son Isaac on the altar?

You see that his faith and his actions were working together, and his faith was made complete by what he did. (James 2:18–22)

Notice the key phrase: "working together." Faith and actions aren't separate—they're partners. They work together. Your hands complete what your mind knows, your heart believes, and your mouth declares.

This isn't about earning salvation through good works. It's about faith naturally expressing itself through action. Would you roast coffee beans but never grind and brew them? Why not release their full potential? Likewise, when faith is real, it will move your hands to serve, to give, to help, and to heal.

Habitual

Finally, biblical faith is habitual. It moves from your head, to your heart, to your mouth, to your hands, and finally to your *feet* as you walk daily with Jesus.

Faith is often talked about as a decision, a point in time when we "accepted Jesus." But the essence of biblical faith is movement, not a moment. It's not just when we started walking with Jesus; it's that we continue to walk with Him.

Jesus speaks of that habitual movement forward by saying, "Whoever wants to be my disciple must deny themselves and take up their cross *daily* and *follow me*" (Luke 9:23, emphasis mine).

Paul put it this way:

> So then, just as you received Christ Jesus as Lord, *continue to live your lives in him*, rooted and built up in him, strengthened in the faith as you were taught, and overflowing with thankfulness. (Colossians 2:6–7, emphasis mine)

Peter adds, "To this you were called, because Christ suffered for you, leaving you an example, that you should *follow in his steps*" (1 Peter 2:21, emphasis mine).

Take up your cross daily. Continue to live your lives in Him. Follow in His steps. This is present tense, ongoing, habitual faith. It's a daily choice to follow when the path is unclear. It's choosing yes over no, trust over control, surrender over stubbornness, again and again. Some days it's effortless; other days it feels impossible. But we keep placing one foot in front of the other as we follow Him.

This is why we call it a "faith journey." Because faith is less about reaching a destination and more about learning to walk after Jesus, at His pace, along the Anchored Path, for the rest of your life.

An Intoxicating Aroma

There's something about the coffee *roasting* process I didn't mention at the start of this chapter: it's not pleasant. Smoke fills the air, and it smells like a concoction of wet hay and burnt popcorn.[44] (That's why I no longer roast and instead purchase freshly roasted beans from one of Colorado's many roasters!)

The smell of *brewing* coffee is different. If Patty starts brewing a batch while I'm still in bed, the intoxicating aroma wakes me up and draws me to the kitchen for that first cup.

In the same way, our transformed, faith-filled lives spread the fragrance of Christ wherever we go. Paul described it this way:

> But thanks be to God, who always leads us as captives in Christ's triumphal procession and uses us to spread the aroma of the knowledge of him everywhere. For we are to God the pleasing aroma of Christ among those who are being saved and those who are perishing. To the one we are an aroma that brings death; to the other, an aroma that brings life. (2 Corinthians 2:14–16)

Full-Bodied Faith

In the previous chapter, we discussed repentance. It's not pleasant, but it's essential. Just as beans must be roasted and ground before they can make coffee, so we must be broken and humbled before we can be filled with new life. Repentance prepares us—it opens us up to receive what God wants to pour in.

In this chapter, we've talked about faith. It starts in our head, moves to our heart, flows from our mouth, works through our hands, and carries our feet forward (figure 9.2). Just as water transforms grounds into an incredible cup of coffee, real faith is transformational—it touches every part of who we are, creating something entirely new. "Therefore, if anyone is in Christ, the new creation has come: The old has gone, the new is here!" (2 Corinthians 5:17).

Have you experienced this kind of full-bodied faith —one that, like brewed coffee, is the result of something ordinary being transformed into something extraordinary?

A Prayer Of Faith

If the following words express what's in your heart, make it your prayer of faith, or use them as a starting point for your own prayer:

> Lord Jesus, I believe You exist (Hebrews 11:6), and that You died for our sins according to the Scriptures, that You were buried, and that You were raised on the third day (1 Corinthians 15:3–4).
>
> More than belief in Your existence, I declare that You are the Messiah, the Son of the living God (Matthew 16:16), and that You are my Lord (Romans 10:9). For it is with my heart that I believe and am justified, and it is with my mouth that I profess my faith and am saved (Romans 10:10).
>
> Your Word says that faith without deeds is dead (James 2:26), so help my faith and actions work together consistently (James 2:22).
>
> I choose today to become Your disciple. Help me deny myself, take up my cross daily, and follow You (Luke 9:23).
>
> In Your name I pray, Amen.[45]

Questions For Reflection

1. Faith starts with acknowledging Jesus actually existed and moves to personally trusting who He is and what He did. Where are you on that journey?

2. "The mouth speaks what the heart is full of" (Matthew 12:34). What feelings arise when you consider declaring your faith—excitement, fear, uncertainty? What does that reveal about your head-to-heart-to-mouth journey?

3. James says faith and actions "work together." Where did your faith show up in your hands this week? Where might God be inviting you to act next?

4. Faith is habitual. What specific practices sustain your daily walk—especially on hard days? How has your view shifted from a one-time decision to an ongoing journey?

5. Christians are called to be "the pleasing aroma of Christ" (2 Corinthians 2:15). Who has been that aroma for you? How might God use your transformed life to draw others?

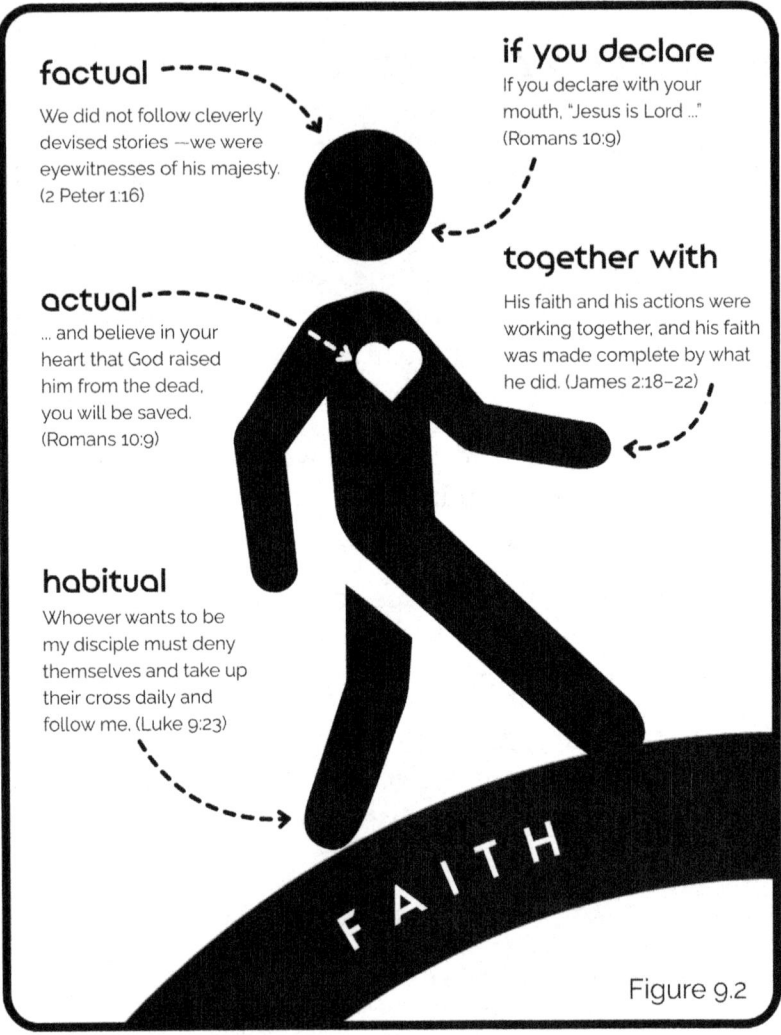

Figure 9.2

10. THE SHAPE OF BELIEVING

I have declared to both Jews and Greeks that they must turn to God in repentance and have faith in our Lord Jesus. (Acts 20:21)

The mountain road curved sharply ahead, with only a guardrail between my school bus and a several-hundred-foot drop. Twenty kids chatted behind me, oblivious to the concentration needed to navigate these switchbacks 1,907 feet above the already mile-high city of Boulder. These conditions are why Colorado has one of the best bus driver training programs in the country—and why our instructor Jack's final words to my cohort of new drivers had been so simple yet so crucial.

I'd started driving bus to earn extra money—both my daughters got married in 2025, and weddings aren't cheap. But what began as a temporary side job became an unexpected lesson in spiritual leadership.

For weeks, Jack had drilled us on everything: pre-trip inspections, student management, chaining up, emergency procedures. We'd practiced navigating these mountain roads until every turn felt familiar. Not all drivers got "mountain trained," but those who did learned to respect the beauty and danger of piloting a 40-foot vehicle through Colorado's peaks.

On the last day of our training, Jack sat the three of us down. After all the PowerPoints, practice drives, and emergency drills, I expected some lengthy final instruction. Instead, he looked us in the eye and said simply: "Don't get complacent."

That was it. Three words. Jack knew the real danger wasn't in what we didn't know—it was in forgetting to apply what we did know. Stay focused. Remember your training. Don't let routine lull you into complacency. If we could do that, our kids would get to home and school safely.

The responsibility of safely guiding others through treacherous terrain isn't limited to mountain roads. As I navigated those switchbacks, I thought of another leader who understood the weight of precious cargo—the Apostle Paul.

Paul's Final Lesson

Reading Paul's farewell to the Ephesian elders in Acts 20, I recognized the same gravity I'd felt on the final day of training. Like Jack with his newly trained drivers, Paul was about to release his spiritual protégés into the world. After nearly three years of intensive discipleship—far

10. THE SHAPE OF BELIEVING

more thorough than my 8 weeks of bus training—he had one essential reminder to leave with them.

Picture the scene: The port city of Miletus, ocean air heavy with the smell of fish and sea spray. Paul had urgently summoned the Ephesian church leaders to meet him here, knowing he'd never see them again. As his weathered hands gripped theirs one final time on that beach, he looked each man in the eye:

> You know that I have not hesitated to preach anything that would be helpful to you but have taught you publicly and from house to house. I have declared to both Jews and Greeks that they must turn to God in repentance and have faith in our Lord Jesus. (Acts 20:21)

Repentance And Faith

There it was—his entire message distilled to its essence. Like Jack's warning against complacency, Paul knew the greatest danger wasn't complexity but forgetting the fundamentals: repentance and faith.

The men on that beach had heard him say it a thousand ways, watched him live it through persecution and praise. It didn't matter who you were, where you came from, or what you had done. The prescription was always the same: turn away from your old life (repent) and turn toward Jesus (faith).

As the ship's captain called for final boarding, the entire group fell to their knees on the sand. Grown men wept openly, clinging to Paul, bidding him farewell. This wasn't just goodbye to a friend—it was the end of a chapter that changed everything.

Paul finally pulled himself away and boarded the ship. The Ephesian elders stayed on the beach long after the sail disappeared, the weight of his words settling in their hearts. They now carried the responsibility to share that same message: "turn to God in repentance and have faith in our Lord Jesus" (Acts 20:21).

The Shape Of Believing

Now we have the full picture of what it looks like to believe (figure 10.1). In Chapter 7, we explored the gap between us and God—a chasm we have no ability to walk across on our own. Our sin, our brokenness, our inability to save ourselves creates an impossible divide. Jesus bridged that gap through His death on the cross and His resurrection.

Figure 10.1

Our image is this: the cross becomes our bridge, and walking across it requires two essential movements.

> REPENT (Chapter 8). Repentance is like the downward arrow on the left. We humble

ourselves, acknowledge our need, and let go of our old life.

FAITH (Chapter 9). Faith is like the upward arrow on the right. We reach up to grasp what God offers, trusting His promises, stepping into new life.

These aren't one-time actions. REPENT and FAITH become the rhythm of the Christian life. We continually turn from sin and turn toward Jesus. We daily die to ourselves and rise to new life. The bridge becomes the path we walk.

Paul's message on that beach echoes through the centuries. Whether you're a lifelong church member or someone who randomly picked up this book, the message is the same: turn to God in repentance and have faith in our Lord Jesus.

Believing Leads To Becoming

But here's the beautiful part—crossing that bridge isn't the end of the Anchored Path. We're just getting started. Because believing leads to becoming—our next Anchor.

If repentance and faith change us, what are we becoming? If belief gets us across the bridge, what happens on the other side? How does the cycle of turning away and turning toward transform us into something new?

The Ephesian elders would discover the answer as they lived out Paul's teaching in the years to come. They would be transformed from the inside out, becoming people who looked increasingly like the One they followed. They would learn that believing isn't a destination—it's the ancient pathway to *becoming*.

That's where we're headed next.

Questions For Reflection:

1. Jack warned against complacency after weeks of training. Where are you most tempted to switch to "autopilot" in your walk with Jesus?

2. Paul's message was identical for everyone. What does this say about the universal nature of our need for God?

3. Repentance and faith are a daily rhythm. Which movement is harder for you right now—and what practices help you sustain it?

4. Consider the image of the cross as a bridge with two movements: REPENT and have FAITH. How does this visual help you understand what it means to believe?

5. As we prepare to explore the Become Anchor, what areas of your life do you sense God wanting to transform through this rhythm of turning away and turning toward?

ANCHOR THREE: BECOME

God loves you just the way you are, but He refuses to leave you that way. He wants you to be just like Jesus.[46] — Max Lucado

As believers, we are not trying to become saints; we are saints who are becoming like Christ.[47] — Neil T Anderson

I press on to take hold of that for which Christ Jesus took hold of me… I do not consider myself yet to have taken hold of it. But one thing I do: Forgetting what is behind and straining toward what is ahead, I press on toward the goal…[48] – Saint Paul

11. THE SHAPE OF BECOMING

And now what are you waiting for? Get up, be baptized and wash your sins away, calling on his name. (Acts 22:16)

The mountain path was steep and hidden, winding through the hills of northern China. Jiang walked beside me, quiet but determined. We were looking for something specific—a place where the mountain stream pooled deep enough for what we'd come to do.

In China, baptism isn't a casual Sunday morning event with family taking photos. It's often a costly declaration affecting your job, your education, and your family relationships. Jiang knew this. That's why we were hiking into the mountains, away from watching eyes, to find a secluded place for him to declare his new life in Christ.

When we found the pool—crystal clear mountain water collecting between the rocks—Jiang smiled. "This is perfect," he said in Mandarin.

As I plunged him below the waters of that cold mountain stream, I thought about all the secret baptisms throughout history—early Christians being baptized in rivers at night, believers in hostile territories finding hidden pools and quiet shores. This wasn't just a ritual; it was Jiang's declaration that his old life was buried with Christ and a new life had begun.

But not all baptisms in China happen in hidden mountain creeks. Sometimes they happen in the heart of the city, in the most common of places.

A few months after Jiang's baptism, I found myself in our neighbor's cramped apartment bathroom, kneeling beside a bathtub. Lily, an 80-year-old woman who'd believed in Jesus for decades, gripped my arm with surprising strength. She had survived the Cultural Revolution, worshipped in secret for years, and now—finally—was ready for this moment she had anticipated her whole life. Her family, a mix of believers and non-believers, crowded in the doorway, watching with curiosity and respect.

"I've waited so long for this," she whispered in Mandarin, tears streaming down her weathered face.

As I helped lower her into the warm water of her bathtub, I thought about how baptism finds a way—in mountain rivers, in bathtubs—wherever hearts are ready to make their declaration.

The Book Of Acts

To understand baptism's significance in the Christian

journey, I often turn to the Book of Acts. I try to read it at least once a year because I love how it's full of stories detailing how ordinary folk cooperated with the Holy Spirit to bring people to Jesus.

My favorite is the story of Philip being sent to share with an Ethiopian eunuch in chapter 8:

> Now an angel of the Lord said to Philip, "Go south to the road—the desert road—that goes down from Jerusalem to Gaza."
>
> So he started out, and on his way he met an Ethiopian eunuch, an important official in charge of all the treasury of the Kandake (which means "queen of the Ethiopians"). This man had gone to Jerusalem to worship, and on his way home was sitting in his chariot reading the Book of Isaiah the prophet.
>
> The Spirit told Philip, "Go to that chariot and stay near it."
>
> Then Philip ran up to the chariot and heard the man reading Isaiah the prophet. "Do you understand what you are reading?" Philip asked.
>
> "How can I," he said, "unless someone explains it to me?" So he invited Philip to come up and sit with him.
>
> This is the passage of Scripture the eunuch was reading: "He was led like a sheep to the slaughter, and as a lamb before its shearer is silent, so he did not open his mouth. In his humiliation he was deprived of justice. Who can

speak of his descendants? For his life was taken from the earth."

The eunuch asked Philip, "Tell me, please, who is the prophet talking about, himself or someone else?"

Then Philip began with that very passage of Scripture and told him the good news about Jesus.

As they traveled along the road, they came to some water and the eunuch said, "Look, here is water. What can stand in the way of my being baptized?"

Philip said, "If you believe with all your heart, you may."

The eunuch answered, "I believe that Jesus Christ is the Son of God."[49]

And he gave orders to stop the chariot. Then both Philip and the eunuch went down into the water and Philip baptized him. (Acts 8:26–38)

There are several things I love about this passage. First, I appreciate how Philip led with curiosity. Rather than assuming the eunuch had no comprehension of what he was reading, Philip asked a question: "Do you understand what you are reading?" (Acts 8:22).

Second, I love the result of Philip's curiosity. The eunuch welcomed Philip into the chariot and basically said, "The only way I can understand this is with someone's guidance" (Acts 8:31).

Philip accepted the invitation, heard the passage the eunuch was reading, and then "began with that very passage of Scripture and told him the good news about Jesus" (Acts 8:35).

If only we had the details of that conversation! Was it minutes? Hours? We'll never know—yet clearly a talk on the need for baptism was part of it, because as soon as they came to water, the eunuch asked, "What can stand in the way of my being baptized?" (Acts 8:36).

Here's what I love most of all: in one conversation, the eunuch experienced all three anchors we've been discussing. The Belong Anchor (through Philip's warm curiosity, "Do you understand?"), the Believe Anchor (when he declared, "I believe that Jesus Christ is the Son of God"), and the Become Anchor (asking, "What can stand in the way of my being baptized?").

Jiang and Lily were ready, too. Despite the risks, they knew that a decision to follow Jesus leads to a decision to be like Jesus. Believing flows toward becoming. The cross leads to water.

The Shape Of Becoming

To understand this progression from believing to becoming, let's look at the symbolism embedded in the act of baptism itself. The waters of baptism will be our canvas for the shape of becoming (figure 11.1).

11. THE SHAPE OF BECOMING

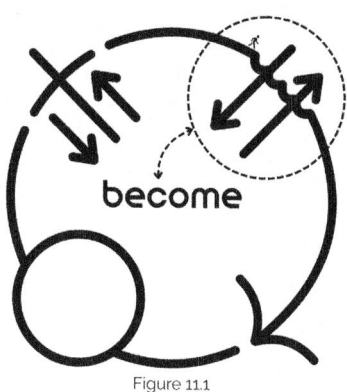

Figure 11.1

Picture yourself standing before these waters. Now visualize two arrows in the water: on the left, an arrow labeled BURIED going down into the water, and on the right, an arrow labeled RAISED coming out of the water (figure 11.2).

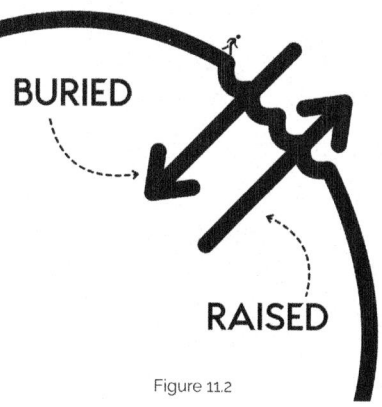

Figure 11.2

These words—BURIED and RAISED—represent the profound reality Paul describes in Romans:

> We were therefore buried with him through baptism into death in order that, just as Christ was raised from the dead through the glory of the Father, we too may live a new life. (Romans

6:4)

What exactly happens in these waters? First, our old life is BURIED. As Paul writes to the Galatians:

> I have been crucified with Christ and I no longer live, but Christ lives in me. The life I now live in the body, I live by faith in the Son of God, who loved me and gave himself for me. (Galatians 2:20)

We'll explore this dying-to-self more deeply in Chapter 12.

Second, a new life is RAISED. Paul declares to the Corinthians: "Therefore, if anyone is in Christ, the new creation has come: The old has gone, the new is here!" (2 Corinthians 5:17). This new creation will be our focus in Chapter 13.

I appreciate how David Pawson expresses it:

> Baptism marks the end of the old life and the beginning of a new life, the death of a sinner and the birth of a saint, the burial of the old man and the resurrection of the new man. It is the "bath of regeneration," bringing about not just a new start in life but a new life to start with![50]

A New Life To Start With

Every baptism—whether in a mountain stream, a bathtub, or a Middle Eastern river—is a decision to be "buried with [Jesus] through baptism" and to be "raised from the dead" to "live a new life" (Romans 6:4).

Have you been baptized? Have you embraced this reality of being buried and raised with Christ? Whether you answer yes, no, or are unsure of what it all means, the next two chapters will further explain this transformation.

Questions For Reflection

1. Philip approached the Ethiopian with curiosity. Think of someone in your life who might be spiritually open. How could you connect them to the Belong Anchor through questions rather than answers?

2. The Ethiopian moved from Belong to Believe to Become in one chariot ride, asking "What can stand in the way of my being baptized?" If you haven't been baptized, what honestly hinders you? Is it fear, not understanding its meaning, waiting for the "right time," or something else? Name it specifically.

3. In baptism, our old life is BURIED, and a new life is RAISED. As you prepare to read chapters 12 and 13, consider: What needs to be buried, and what are you ready to see God raise to life?

12. BURIED WITH CHRIST

> *For you were buried with Christ when you were baptized. And with him you were raised to new life because you trusted the mighty power of God, who raised Christ from the dead.* (Colossians 2:12, NLT)

The small church smelled like old wood, tattered hymnals, and decades of potlucks. I'd slipped away from the pre-concert chatter, needing a moment alone before our small choir performed that night. Sitting in a hard wooden pew, I couldn't shake what I'd just overheard.

It was the fall of 1991, our first semester of Bible college. Patty had been talking with the music director of our eight-voice group about her parents' divorce. She was twelve when it happened—the same age I was when my parents split. I was already attracted to Patty, but hearing her describe that familiar ache made something shift inside me. It wasn't just attraction anymore. It was being known—like looking at someone and seeing your own story reflected back.

I hadn't meant to eavesdrop, which is why I'd retreated to the empty sanctuary. But sitting there in the quiet, my hidden pain surfaced. The divorce. The confusion. The way a twelve-year-old tries to make sense of a family falling apart.

Then, something unexpected happened.

In that simple church, on that worn pew, I had a vision of Jesus on the cross. I heard Him speak, too. Not audibly, but unmistakably clear: "When I went to the cross, I didn't just take on all the sin of the world. I also took on all the pain. Not just your pain, but everyone's pain. And when I rose from the grave, I not only left behind all the sin, but I left all that hurt in the grave, too. You don't have to keep living with it."

I sat there stunned. All my life, I'd understood the cross as God's solution for *sin*. Forgiveness. Redemption. A clean slate. And that's absolutely true—sin is the core issue.

But this? This was expanding my understanding. Jesus hadn't just died for what I'd done wrong. He also took on Himself the wrong that had been done to *me*—crucifying and burying both my wickedness and my wounds.

In the previous chapter, I shared a verse from Paul that speaks of this burial:

> For we died and were buried with Christ by baptism. And just as Christ was raised from the dead by the glorious power of the Father, now we also may live new lives. (Romans 6:4, NLT)

He wrote about that same burial to the Colossians:

> For you were buried with Christ when you were baptized. And with him you were raised to new life because you trusted the mighty power of God, who raised Christ from the dead. (Colossians 2:12, NLT)

That evening at the church, I began to understand just how complete our burial needs to be. Yes, our sins get buried—that's the foundation. But the burial goes deeper than I'd realized. It's about allowing every broken, idolatrous, and destructive part of our old life to be put to death and laid in the tomb with Jesus.

Under the baptismal waters, we're not just getting wet. We're participating in a funeral—our own. Everything that defined our old life gets buried with Christ. And just as Jesus left sin and death in the tomb, we leave our sins and wounds in the waters.

Let me show you the full picture of what goes under using the letters of BURIED.

Brokenness And Pain

As I sat on the pew that evening, the first thing I learned is that we must allow our brokenness and pain to be taken to the cross and buried alongside our sin. Jesus doesn't just forgive; He heals. I hear that promise in one of David's psalms: "The Lord is close to the brokenhearted and saves those who are crushed in spirit" (Psalm 34:18).

When we examined the Believe Anchor in the previous section, we came to understand that Jesus forgives our sin. But David's song confirms that Jesus also draws near to our broken hearts, and He heals our crushed spirits. Have you allowed your hurts to be dealt with, too? To be genuinely healed and not simply ignored?

Consider Isaiah's prophecy about Jesus:

> Surely he took up our pain and bore our suffering, yet we considered him punished by God, stricken by him, and afflicted. But he was pierced for our transgressions, he was crushed for our iniquities; the punishment that brought us peace was on him, and by his wounds we are healed. (Isaiah 53:4–5)

Pierced for our pain. Punished for our peace. Wounded for our healing.

What a relief when my 18-year-old self realized I didn't need to cling to my brokenness and pain anymore. Jesus had taken it with Him to the grave. And when He rose, He didn't bring it back.

As I allowed those emotional wounds to be healed, I realized something else had to be dealt with: my bitterness and unforgiveness.

Unforgiveness

For six years, I'd been carrying something heavy: unforgiveness. In my twelve-year-old logic, when my parents divorced, someone had to be at fault. Since Mom was the one who left, she became the target of my bitterness.

I didn't see it as unforgiveness. To me, it was justified anger. Unfair hurt. I labeled it a lot of things except what it really was—a bitter root poisoning me from the inside out.

Here's what I began learning in that season of my life: when Jesus took on my brokenness and pain on the cross—my sin of unforgiveness was heaped on Him, too. My grudge against my mom was draped around His shoulders.

And then He took all of that to the grave. Why then was I still holding on? You can almost hear Paul losing patience for this tendency of ours when he writes:

> Get rid of all bitterness, rage and anger, brawling and slander, along with every form of malice. Be kind and compassionate to one another, forgiving each other, just as in Christ God forgave you. (Ephesians 4:31-32)

Notice the order. First, we experience God's love and forgiveness. (That's why the Anchors of Belong and Believe come first). We are then empowered to extend that same forgiveness to others.

I couldn't forgive my mom until I understood Christ's love and forgiveness. I couldn't release her from my judgment until I realized Jesus had released me from His. I couldn't let go of my bitterness until I understood my brokenness and unforgiveness had been crucified and buried in the grave.

Jesus told a story about forgiveness. I'd like you to read it in its entirety:

> Therefore, the kingdom of heaven is like a king who wanted to settle accounts with his

servants. As he began the settlement, a man who owed him ten thousand bags of gold was brought to him. Since he was not able to pay, the master ordered that he and his wife and his children and all that he had be sold to repay the debt. At this the servant fell on his knees before him.

"Be patient with me," he begged, "and I will pay back everything."

The servant's master took pity on him, canceled the debt and let him go.

But when that servant went out, he found one of his fellow servants who owed him a hundred silver coins. He grabbed him and began to choke him.

"Pay back what you owe me!" he demanded.

His fellow servant fell to his knees and begged him, "Be patient with me, and I will pay it back."

But he refused. Instead, he went off and had the man thrown into prison until he could pay the debt.

When the other servants saw what had happened, they were outraged and went and told their master everything that had happened. Then the master called the servant in.

"You wicked servant," he said, "I canceled all that debt of yours because you begged me to. Shouldn't you have had mercy on your fellow servant just as I had on you?"

> In anger his master handed him over to the jailers to be tortured, until he should pay back all he owed.
>
> This is how my heavenly Father will treat each of you unless you forgive your brother or sister from your heart. (Matthew 18:23–35)

My mom didn't owe me ten thousand bags of gold or a hundred silver coins. But in my young heart, she owed me an intact family. She owed me explanations. She owed me something I couldn't quite name but desperately wanted back.

Who is it for you? Who or what caused the hurt? From whom do you feel justified in withholding forgiveness? Can you visualize yourself burying your unforgiveness in the grave—and allowing it to remain there?

Learning to forgive my mom—and choosing to love her again—didn't happen instantly. But it started as I sat in that pew and realized that my unforgiveness had to be buried with Christ. The hurt. The blame. The narrative I'd been telling myself about whose fault it was. I began to let it be buried with Him.

Reign Of Sin

Unforgiveness is like a 900-pound sin-gorilla. As the Lord helped (and continues to help) me bury that beast, I've discovered it sits on something just as heavy—the reign and rule of sin itself.

Our brokenness and unforgiveness act like blinders, preventing us from seeing how sin rules other areas of our lives. When we're focused on our wounds or nursing our grudges, we can become blind to sin's quiet control elsewhere. It's like having a broken bone that hurts so much, you don't notice the infection spreading in another part of your body.

Jesus said:

> For if you forgive other people when they sin against you, your heavenly Father will also forgive you. But if you do not forgive others their sins, your Father will not forgive your sins. (Matthew 6:14–15)

Your sins. Plural.

Brokenness and unforgiveness cloud our vision, so it's crucial to address them first. As we allow them to be buried (and healed), we can begin to see how sin has been secretly reigning in other areas of our life.

After my parents' divorce, my bitterness toward my mom was just the presenting problem. It sat on top of other sins ruling my life.

Lust was one of those sins. In the 80s, it was harder to do, but I still found a way to view porn. It provided momentary comfort, but left me feeling unclean and empty.

Fornication was another. It's the sin we share with someone—compounding the effects of sin, guilt, and shame. All while holding out the hope that it will make us feel better. It doesn't.

Anger and envy were present. I did a pretty good job of keeping them inside, but I could sure cut someone down with the words I spoke to them in my mind.

Hypocrisy crept in too. I learned to wear different masks—the dutiful Christian around church folks, while showing a completely different face to my other friends.

Bottom line? Sin rules and reigns in us—until we let Jesus bury it. Consider this passage:

> The death he died, he died to sin once for all; but the life he lives, he lives to God. In the same way, count yourselves dead to sin but alive to God in Christ Jesus.
>
> Therefore do not let sin reign in your mortal body so that you obey its evil desires. Do not offer any part of yourself to sin as an instrument of wickedness, but rather offer yourselves to God as those who have been brought from death to life; and offer every part of yourself to him as an instrument of righteousness.
>
> For sin shall no longer be your master, because you are not under the law, but under grace. (Romans 6:10–14)

The Bible wouldn't say we could do it if it couldn't be done. Sin doesn't have to reign. Temptation doesn't get to control. Satan doesn't have a right to be your master. "The death [Jesus] died, he died to sin once for all" (Romans 6:10).

This doesn't mean we'll never make another mistake (I wish!). But it means sin no longer rules us or has the final word. As Paul celebrates: "Thanks be to God, who delivers me through Jesus Christ our Lord!" (Romans 7:25).

I hate to say it, but we're not done yet. As I've already mentioned, certain sins aren't obvious to us due to the blindness caused by brokenness and unforgiveness.

Other sins remain hidden ... because we *love* them.

Idolatry

That same freshman year of Bible college, God pointed out something else to bury. It lived in my dorm room, organized alphabetically in thick black binders—my beloved CD collection.

I'd spent years building it. There were hundreds of discs. Some bought with newspaper-delivery money, others received as gifts, each carefully placed in its protective sleeve. It was more than music to me. It was my escape. My identity. My way of controlling my world after my parents' divorce.

The problem wasn't the music itself (well, not all of it). The problem was what it had become. When I was angry, I didn't seek God—I turned up my stereo. When I was lonely, I didn't reach out to others—I disappeared into the disc jacket, reading every lyric. The words of these songs shaped my thoughts more than Scripture. The artists influenced my worldview more than Jesus.

I'd made music my refuge. And in His kindness, God was showing me that anything we run to before Him is an idol. No wonder John's final words in his first letter to the church pleaded, "Dear children, keep yourselves from idols" (1 John 5:21).

During a college chapel service, I heard God ask: "Will you

surrender this to me?"

It wasn't about the CDs being evil, but what they'd become—a god with a lowercase 'g'. Something I treasured more than I treasured Him. Something that influenced my emotions and thoughts more than He did.

John Calvin wrote, "The human mind is, so to speak, a perpetual forge of idols."[51] He observed that we constantly manufacture substitutes for God. Success. Relationships. Comfort. Control. Even good things can become ultimate things and thus become idols.

That night, I went through my collection. Most CDs I got rid of. A few I kept, but with a different perspective. My greatly reduced collection was no longer my identity or refuge. What remained would serve to support my growing relationship with God.

In baptism, we drown our idols—things we've elevated above God, substitutes for His presence, and lowercase 'g' gods. They get buried in the tomb—never to be raised.

What are your idols that need to be buried?

Embarrassment, Guilt, And Shame

Dealing with sin can be embarrassing.

> "I held on to my brokenness for that long?"
> "I was that unforgiving?"
> "I got involved in that sin?"
> "I served those idols?"

We start in victory, allowing our sin and hurt to be buried with Christ. Then, we are accosted by embarrassment, guilt, and shame. "I can't believe what a fool I was."

We're tempted to keep it inside. "If anyone knew my past, they'd look down on me. I'd lose their respect. I must keep this as my shameful secret."

My pew experience happened early in the school year, giving me an opportunity. I could allow my brokenness, unforgiveness, sin, and idolatry to be buried with Christ —yet hold on to my private embarrassment—or I could bring it *all* into the light.

As our group traveled to churches, we took turns sharing between songs. I don't know if my fellow vocalists got tired of it, but concert after concert, I began telling my story—the divorce, the bitterness, the hypocrisy, the healing. The very things that embarrassed me became my testimony.

You know what I discovered? Speaking it out didn't increase my shame—it dissolved it. I should have known this! David wrote that confessing our sin doesn't curse us. It blesses us:

> Blessed is the one whose transgressions are forgiven, whose sins are covered. Blessed is the one whose sin the LORD does not count against them and in whose spirit is no deceit.
>
> When I kept silent, my bones wasted away through my groaning all day long... Then I acknowledged my sin to you and did not cover up my iniquity. I said, "I will confess my transgressions to the LORD." And you forgave the guilt of my sin. (Psalm 32:1-5)

Understand this: Satan loves to dig up what God has buried. He's like a prosecuting attorney who keeps bringing up evidence that's been thrown out of court.

> "Remember when you ..."
> "Don't forget about ..."
> "How could you have ..."

You know how you can respond? "You're right. Thanks for the reminder, but I'm no longer embarrassed. I'm going to tell someone the story of how God has changed me."

Here's the truth: our testimony has power not in spite of our past, but because of it. When we share how God transformed our brokenness into beauty, our shame loses its grip. The things meant to embarrass us become evidence of God's grace. As Jesus was placed in the tomb, our embarrassment, guilt, and shame can be buried too.

"Those who look to him are radiant," David writes. "Their faces are never covered with shame" (Psalm 34:5).

Deception

The last thing to be buried might be the most dangerous —deception. In *A Deeper Walk*, Marcus Warner writes:

> The devil's lies interpret our pain. He tells us that God has abandoned us and cannot be trusted. He tells us that we are worthless and alone. He tells us lies that feel true because of the pain we have experienced.[52]

I experienced this in the years following my parents'

divorce. I believed demonic lies. Subtle deceptions somehow felt true:

> "You're damaged goods."
> "God can't use someone with your background."
> "You'll probably repeat your parents' mistakes."

Even in my senior year of college, I remember giving voice to a lie I had been rehearsing in my head. I was alone in our trailer (Patty and I were married after our sophomore year). In the dark of our living room, I said out loud to myself, "You'll never amount to anything." In my mind, I knew those words were false. But in my heart, they somehow felt true.

My experience illustrates that deception often begins with a wound. Isn't that awful? We get wounded—then the enemy comes in and translates it, giving the wound a hellish meaning:

> "No one cares."
> "God hates me."
> "I'm worthless."
> "I'll never amount to anything."

Don't be surprised. This is what the deceiver does. Lies are his "native language" (John 8:44) and he's particularly skilled at making them feel true.

This is why Warner warns against asking, "What lies did I start to believe after I was wounded?" He suggests we instead ask, "What started *feeling* true after this wound happened?"[53]

Ask yourself that right now. What started feeling true after the wound? As you discover the answer to that—

you'll likely expose the lie you've been believing. What do you do with that lie? I think you know by now. Let it be crucified and buried along with all the sin and hurt from your old life.

As I shared my story concert after concert, I wasn't just dissolving shame. I was taking deception and lies to the cross. Each time I spoke the truth about God's healing and forgiveness, another demonic deception lost its power.

Buried.

"For you were buried with Christ when you were baptized..." (Colossians 2:12a, NLT).

> Brokenness and pain buried.
> Unforgiveness buried.
> Reign of sin buried.
> Idolatry buried.
> Embarrassment, guilt, and shame buried.
> Deception buried.

All of it dies and goes into the grave with Christ. Not ignored, minimized, or forgotten. It's buried with Christ. Destructive stuff dies and bullying voices get buried. The old life, with its wounds and lies, gets sealed in the tomb —and we become free, truly free.

> It is for freedom that Christ has set us free. Stand firm, then, and do not let yourselves be burdened again by a yoke of slavery. (Galatians 5:1)

And here's the best news of all: the story doesn't end in a tomb. Read again the second half of the verses we read at the beginning:

> And just as Christ was raised from the dead by the glorious power of the Father, now we also may live new lives. (Romans 6:4b, NLT)

> And with him you were raised to new life because you trusted the mighty power of God, who raised Christ from the dead. (Colossians 2:12b, NLT)

That's where we're headed next. Resurrection!

Just as Christ was raised from the dead, what does God's Spirit want to raise to life in you?

A Prayer Of Freedom

If the following words resonate with you, pray them as your own declaration of freedom—or let them guide you toward your own prayer:

> *Lord Jesus, surely You took up my pain and bore my suffering (Isaiah 53:4), so today I let it go. The brokenness, hurt, wounds, and pain—I give them all to you.*

> *In Jesus name, I get rid of all unforgiveness, bitterness, rage, and anger. I forgive others, just as in Christ God forgave me (Ephesians 4:31-32).*

> *I count myself dead to sin but alive to God in Christ Jesus, and I do not let sin reign in me or obey its evil desires. I offer myself to God, and sin shall no longer be my master (Romans 6:11–14).*

With Your help, I keep myself from idols (1 John 5:21). Help me identify them, surrender them to You, and bury them.

I give You all my embarrassment, guilt, and shame. The punishment that brings me peace was on You, and by Your wounds I am healed (Isaiah 53:5).

I no longer let the enemy interpret my pain. He is a liar and the father of all lies (John 8:44) and with Your help, I will know the truth, and the truth will set me free (John 8:32).

For I was buried with Christ when I was baptized (Colossians 2:12), and it is for freedom that Christ has set me free. I stand firm, and will not let myself be burdened again by a yoke of slavery (Galatians 5:1).

Brokenness buried. Unforgiveness buried. Reign of sin buried. Idolatry buried. Embarrassment buried. Deception buried.

In Jesus's name, Amen.[54]

Questions For Reflection

1. In a quiet moment, name the specific pain or brokenness you've been carrying. Will you invite Jesus to heal it—and picture Him taking your hurt to the cross?

2. Who do you need to forgive? Name the person and the wound. What step will you take this week to bury bitterness with Christ (prayer, conversation, or release)?

3. What do you run to before you run to God—success, comfort, control, a habit, or a hobby? Identify one "good

thing" that's become an ultimate thing, and surrender it.

4. Using Marcus Warner's framing: After your wound, what started feeling true? Write the lie, cross it out, then write God's truth next to it—and speak that truth aloud.

5. What part of your story is hidden by embarrassment or shame? Identify one safe person or setting where you can share it, so your testimony dissolves shame and strengthens others.

13. RAISED WITH CHRIST

> *I pray that the eyes of your heart may be enlightened in order that you may know the hope to which he has called you, the riches of his glorious inheritance in his holy people, and his incomparably great power for us who believe. (Ephesians 1:18–19)*

It was the spring of 2019. The unopened box sat on the table while my staff watched expectantly. It was my going away party in northern China where I'd served as pastor of an international church, and they'd just presented me with this gift. I knew what was inside—colorblind glasses—and I was terrified.

I was born with Protan color blindness, a type of red-green color vision deficiency that makes the world appear muted to me while others see vibrant reds and greens.

I'd always been curious about these special glasses that promised to reveal colors I'd never truly seen. I'd seen videos of grown men crying as they put them on and assumed it was hype. Sitting there with my team watching, I feared disappointing them. What if I put them on and nothing happened? What if my colorblindness was too severe?

Taking a big breath, I slipped on the glasses.

First, nothing—my fears were realized. Then I noticed our children's pastor's shirt. Was she wearing that earlier? Without thinking, I blurted out, "You wear that in public?" I laughed, trying to soften my outburst. I didn't want to offend her.

Suddenly, what had appeared as a modest, dull color blazed with a vibrancy I'd never experienced. Red—actual red—was almost vulgar in its intensity. It was loud, bright, demanding attention in a way that made me understand why people used "screaming" to describe certain shades.

When I stepped outside, China transformed. Intellectually, I knew the country loves red, but now I could *see* it. Red banners hung over storefronts I'd passed a thousand times. Even some of the crosswalks were painted red. I called Patty: "Did you know some of the crosswalks are *red?*"

Children with red shoes. Women with red scarves. Even through the perpetual smog, the color punched through, announcing itself everywhere I looked. For years, I'd lived in a city painted a color I couldn't see.

Shortly after that party, my family moved to Colorado —"color red" or "ruddy" in Spanish. I'd soon find out why.

On our first mountain hike, I sat on a rock weeping. (The

YouTube videos are real!) Plants I'd thought were dying, their leaves looking brown and lifeless to my colorblind eyes, were actually deep burgundy. They were alive, vibrant, and beautiful.

I held a single leaf. The greens—I had no idea there were so many shades. They'd always been this way. I just couldn't see them.

This experience reminds me of being raised with Christ. Paul writes, "Therefore, if anyone is in Christ, the new creation has come: The old has gone, the new is here!" (2 Corinthians 5:17).

The problem is we're often unaware of this transformation. We're a new creation but don't live like it. We understand the burial has happened, yet we forget we're also raised. We need to take our glasses out of the box and put them on.

I want to help you see what God's Spirit wants to raise to life in you using the letters of RAISED.

Relationship With God

My brother lives on a large piece of land in Florida in a big cabin that's always full of chaos and laughter. He and his wife have five kids—their first son biologically, then four more children through adoption. It's beautiful to see the diversity in their home. One son has tight curly black hair, another has tight curly blonde hair. Different heritages—African, Asian, European—all represented in one family.

What gets me every time is hearing them call my brother "Daddy." Not "Uncle," "Mr. Durbin," or some distance-keeping title. Daddy. Each of them addresses him with the same casual confidence and automatic trust—whether they became his own by way of genes or a judge's decree.

This is what happened when you were raised with Christ. Your relationship with God changed. You became His child. Not metaphorically or poetically. Actually. "Yet to all who did receive him, to those who believed in his name, he gave the right to become children of God" (John 1:12).

Notice the phrase "the right." It's a legal phrase. An adoption phrase. The same right my brother's adopted children have to call him Daddy, carry his last name, and be members of his household.

Neil T. Anderson beautifully captures this in *Victory Over the Darkness*:[55]

> Through Christ, God provided a way for us into His family. As God's adopted children, we have been given a new identity and a new name. We are no longer spiritual orphans; we are sons and daughters of God.

Like my niece and nephews, you might come from a different background than other children in God's family. Your past might look nothing like theirs. Your hangups, hurts, wounds—all different. But as you received Christ and believed in His name, your relationship with God has forever changed.

> The Spirit you received does not make you slaves, so that you live in fear again; rather, the Spirit you received brought about your adoption to sonship. And by him we cry, "Abba, Father."

> The Spirit himself testifies with our spirit that we are God's children. (Romans 8:15–16)

Authority In Christ

Just as my brother's adopted children have the same rights as his biological son, you've been given something more than just a relationship—you've been given authority. I discovered the reality of this authority in 2015 in the most unlikely place: a Chinese nursing home.

My family was visiting residents at the facility. These places carry a particular sadness in China. In a culture where families traditionally care for their elderly at home, these facilities often house those who have been left behind or have no living relatives.

While on the outdoor patio, a nurse escorted an elderly man to me with an unusual request. She explained he'd been dizzy for eleven years. Then came the unexpected question: "What do you suggest for his condition?"

I'm a pastor, not a doctor. "Drink more water?" I offered weakly.

After a pause and considering the risk, I dared to ask if I could pray. The home was government subsidized, and I was offering something "religious." Even as I said it, I wondered if I had overstepped. Would the nurse report me? Would we be asked to leave?

Thankfully, the nurse reluctantly agreed to let me pray. I kept it simple, since my Mandarin was limited: "Dizziness go. Healing come. In Jesus's name. Amen."[56]

When I said, "Amen," the residents were called to dinner.

The nurse escorted the gentleman away, and I thought nothing more of it.

A few minutes later in the cafeteria, the same man came walking—no, striding—back to me. His nurse struggled to keep pace. With her help, his message became clear: He wanted to know the words I'd spoken. What was the magic formula? Could I write them down?

The dizziness was gone. Eleven years of imbalance vanished in a moment.

"It wasn't the words," I told him, still processing what happened. "It's who I was talking to. Jesus has authority over sickness, and He shares that authority with His family—people like me who believe in Him."

Honestly, I hadn't expected this authority to "show up" when I prayed. But why not? When God adopted us, He granted us the right to be His children and to walk in His authority.

What does that authority look like?

It's not just about healing or miraculous signs, though those certainly occur. More fundamentally, it looks like supernatural certainty—not in our own power or perfect prayers—but a confidence in the "name that is above every name" (Philippians 2:9).

The writer of Hebrews says, "Let us then approach God's throne of grace with confidence, so that we may receive mercy and find grace to help us in our time of need" (Hebrews 4:16).

The elderly gentleman didn't need eloquent words or perfect theology. He needed someone who understood their authority *in* Christ—and the authority *of* Christ—even if that someone was still figuring it out!

What would your life look like if you faced your greatest fears, fully convinced that you walk in Christ's authority?

Inheritance

Authority isn't the only thing that comes with being part of God's family. There's also an inheritance.

In 2013, while still living in southern China, Patty had a recurring dream. We inherited a home—not just any, but one filled with tunnels connecting to influential places: government offices, businesses, and corridors of power we'd never accessed. It seemed like just a strange dream.

Then we moved to northern China.

My predecessor at the international church, Pastor Cliff, had a running joke when he introduced me during the year I shadowed him. He would say, "First Paul took my home. Then he took my car. And now he has my job."

Technically, these things didn't "belong" to Pastor Cliff, and I hadn't "taken" them from him, either. But he had been using them, and he willingly entrusted them to me: the home, the car, and the job.

The home was part of a beautiful walled community in the heart of the city. We didn't quite know who our neighbors were, but they seemed important, famous, and connected.

In a matter of months in my role as pastor, I was meeting with government officials, CEOs, and foreign ambassadors. Patty's dream had become our reality—we'd inherited not just a home, but access to places and people we couldn't reach on our own.

This is what it means to be raised with Christ—you've inherited something you didn't work for. Paul writes, "The Spirit himself testifies with our spirit that we are God's children. Now if we are children, then we are heirs—heirs of God and co-heirs with Christ" (Romans 8:16-17).

Heirs of God, and co-heirs with Christ. You inherit what Christ inherits. You have what He has.

> For in Christ all the fullness of the Deity lives in bodily form, and in Christ you have been brought to fullness. He is the head over every power and authority. (Colossians 2:9–10)

His family is your family. His authority is your authority. His home is your home. When Peter contemplated this, he could barely contain his excitement:

> Praise be to the God and Father of our Lord Jesus Christ! In his great mercy he has given us new birth into a living hope through the resurrection of Jesus Christ from the dead, and into an inheritance that can never perish, spoil or fade. (1 Peter 1:3-4)

Our home in the city was an amazing place for our family to live, but just as with any structure, I could already see cracks developing in the walls. One day, bulldozers will flatten those posh residences to build something different.

This is true of all our material possessions and

positions. They will perish, spoil, and fade. But our inheritance in Christ? It remains for eternity. "When you believed, you were marked in him with a seal, the promised Holy Spirit, who is a deposit guaranteeing our inheritance..." (Ephesians 1:13-14).

The question isn't whether you have an inheritance—you do. The real question is whether you're living in it. God has given you keys to a kingdom inheritance that includes peace, purpose, and power for living.

Will you walk through the door?

Sainthood

In the fall of 1999, I was sitting at our living room table in North Dakota with three teen boys from our youth group. We were discussing their identity in Christ when I dropped what I thought would be an encouraging truth: "As followers of Jesus, you're no longer sinners—you're saints."

The look on one boy's face—a mixture of shock and disbelief—is burned into my memory. "No way," he said.

In North Dakota's largely Catholic culture, "saint" meant someone famous and dead. Saint Hallvard. Saint Olaf. People with statues and feast days. Not a sixteen-year-old who just got detention for skipping class.

I understood his reaction; I'd had the same one.

The first time I read Neil T. Anderson's *Victory Over the Darkness*, I was stunned. He writes, "Although the New Testament provides plenty of evidence that believers do sin, it never identifies the believer as a sinner."[57]

As a teen, I sang a theology-forming (and theologically problematic) solo at my church back in Montana where the chorus proclaimed, "I'm just a sinner saved by grace."[58] I thought, "This must be my identity. I'm *just* a *sinner* saved by grace." It never even crossed my mind to think of myself as a saint.

Here's what I wanted those boys to understand—and what I hope you'll understand, too: once a person believes in Jesus, the Bible no longer refers to them as a sinner.

When Paul addressed the highly problematic church in Corinth, he didn't write, "To the troublemakers in Corinth" or "To the spiritual failures in Corinth." Instead, he wrote: "To the church of God that is in Corinth, to those sanctified in Christ Jesus, called to be saints" (1 Corinthians 1:2). Not future saints. Not saints-in-training. Saints right now, despite their struggles.

The boys at our table had it backwards. They thought you had to be good to be called a saint. The truth? They were already saints learning to live like it. Anderson nails it: "As believers, we are not trying to become saints; we are saints who are becoming like Christ."[59]

This is a powerful realization. If we've put our faith in Christ—yet continue to view ourselves as *sinners*—then we should expect to keep on sinning. But if we accept the truth that we are *saints*—our mindsets will shift—and we'll expect to live in the victory that the Bible promises.

> His divine power has given us everything we need for a godly life through our knowledge of him who called us by his own glory and goodness. Through these he has given us

his very great and precious promises, so that through them you may participate in the divine nature, having escaped the corruption in the world caused by evil desires. (2 Peter 1:3–4)

What would it look like to slip on glasses for spiritual color-blindness and view yourself not as "a sinner saved by grace," but as "a sinner saved—*and transformed into a saint*—by grace"?

And not just "saved *by*."

"Saved *for*."

Embark On A Mission

It's autumn of 2025 as I write this. Patty and I just went for a walk, and I made sure to take my colorblind glasses. After six years, you'd think I'd have seen every color by now. But walking in Colorado with my favorite glasses has become a mission—I'm hunting for hues I've still never seen.

Today, I picked up a leaf transitioning from green to red. It made me tear up again. "What colors am I seeing?"

"Tangerine-ish here, tomato-red there, and see this edge? That's dark burgundy."

I pointed at a flower. "What about that?"

"True pink."

"And this one?"

"That's more lilac."

After all this time, I'm still discovering colors that were

always there. Sage, chartreuse, violet, maroon—each of our walks is a mission to see the ones I've been missing.

This is what it means to be raised with Christ. You're not just saved from something; you're saved *for* something. Put it this way: you're not saved to be seated; you're saved to be *sent*. You are a new creation with a new mission.

Alan and Debra Hirsch say,

> You simply cannot be a disciple without being a missionary—a sent one. For way too long discipleship has been limited to issues relating to our own personal morality and worked out in the context of the four walls of the church with its privatized religion.[60]

Being a follower of Christ isn't just about becoming more informed through intellectual study; it's about becoming more in sync with the mission of Jesus.

Consider Paul's words to the Ephesians, and note the things we've already looked at—relationship, authority, inheritance—and how it all leads to a mission.

> But because of his great love for us, God, who is rich in mercy, made us alive with Christ even when we were dead in transgressions—it is by grace you have been saved.
>
> And God raised us up with Christ and seated us with him in the heavenly realms in Christ Jesus, in order that in the coming ages he might show the incomparable riches of his grace, expressed in his kindness to us in Christ Jesus.
>
> For it is by grace you have been saved, through

faith—and this is not from yourselves, it is the gift of God—not by works, so that no one can boast.

For we are God's handiwork, created in Christ Jesus to do good works, which God prepared in advance for us to do. (Ephesians 2:4–10)

There's the mission—we're "created in Christ Jesus to do good works." Here's my paraphrase: we're created to embark on a mission. It's our design, our purpose, the reason He created us.

The colors were always in Colorado, but I needed the glasses to see them. With my new eyes, I find that I can't help but point them out to others. "Do you see that blue spruce? Isn't it amazing?"

Once you see what God has done in your life—once you see the colors of His amazing grace, I pray you'll embark on a mission to make them obvious to others.

What does your mission look like? In time, the Holy Spirit will let you know. What's needed first is your availability and surrender. Will you say with the prophet Isaiah, "Here am I, send me"? (Isaiah 6:8).

Disciple Others

Here are Jesus's departing words to His disciples:

> Therefore go and make disciples of all nations, baptizing them in the name of the Father and of the Son and of the Holy Spirit, and teaching them to obey everything I have commanded you. And surely I am with you always, to the

very end of the age. (Matthew 28:19-20)

Did you notice? Jesus's final command wasn't "Go and attend church" or "Go to another conference." It was "Go and make disciples of all nations."

Make disciples ... sounds like something professionals do, right? I get it. If it helps, think of discipleship as mentoring—guiding someone along the same Anchored Path you've walked. Demonstrate they belong before they believe. Answer questions so belief can take root. Walk with them as they become who God created them to be. Challenge them to do the same for others.

It's not about being perfect. I still can't name the new colors I'm looking at. I just know I'm seeing something wonderful. Discipling others is saying, "Let me show you what I've discovered. Let me help you see what God helped me see."

You don't need a theology degree or all the answers. Just be a step or two ahead on the path, reaching back to help someone else take their next step. Someone helped you belong. Someone explained belief to you. Someone walked with you as you became more like Christ. Now it's your turn to be that someone for another.

This is where the Anchored Path we've traced comes full circle. You've been raised with Christ. You've opened the box and put on the glasses. Now comes the beautiful responsibility—and joy—of helping others see the colors, too.

Preparing To Belay

Guiding others—belaying them—on their climb with Christ is vital to our walk with Jesus. It's what we were made for.

Leaning on His support is just as vital. In his small but mighty book, *Surprise the World!*, Michael Frost writes, "We need to be propelled outward, into the lives of our neighbors, but also upward, into deeper intimacy with Jesus."[61]

Intimacy with Jesus—that's how we'll begin our study of the Belay Anchor.

A Prayer Of Identity

If the following words express what you're discovering, pray them as your "raised" identity declaration—or let them inspire your own unique prayer:

> *Dear Heavenly Father, the Spirit I received from You does not make me a slave, so that I live in fear again; rather, the Spirit I received brought about my adoption (Romans 8:15). I am Your child! (John 1:12).*
>
> *I can now approach Your throne of grace with confidence, so that I may receive mercy and find grace to help me in my time of need (Hebrews 4:16), and You have given me authority to overcome all the power of the enemy; nothing will harm me (Luke 10:19).*
>
> *When I believed, I was marked in You with a seal, the promised Holy Spirit, who is a deposit guaranteeing my inheritance (Ephesians 1:13-14),*

an inheritance that can never perish, spoil or fade (1 Peter 1:4).

I accept the truth that I am a saint (1 Corinthians 1:2), and trust that Your divine power has given me everything I need for a godly life (2 Peter 1:3).

For I am Your handiwork, created in Christ Jesus to do good works, embarking on a mission which You prepared in advance for me to do (Ephesians 2:10).

I will therefore go and make disciples who make disciples, knowing that You are with me always, to the very end of the age (Matthew 28:19-20).

In Jesus's name I pray, Amen.[62]

Questions For Reflection

1. Name one concrete way your relationship with God has changed since following Jesus. How has it shaped your daily life? Have you fully embraced your identity as His child?

2. Where do you need to exercise the authority Christ has given you? What holds you back from walking in that authority?

3. Where are you still striving to earn what's already yours in Christ, and what would it look like to fully receive it this week?

4. If you saw yourself as a saint (not merely a sinner saved by grace), what habit or decision would you change immediately?

5. Who is one person God may be sending you to

this week? What specific first step will you take to come alongside—seeking their permission and offering guidance—and begin discipling/mentoring them?

ANCHOR FOUR: BELAY

The first act of love is always the giving of attention.[63] — Dallas Willard

Do not waste time bothering whether you "love" your neighbor; act as if you did.[64] — C.S. Lewis

For Christ's love compels us, because we are convinced that one died for all, and therefore all died. And he died for all, that those who live should no longer live for themselves but for him who died for them and was raised again.[65] — Saint Paul

14. THE SHAPE OF BELAYING

The words I have spoken to you—they are full of the Spirit and life. (John 6:63)

The farm truck backing into our driveway meant only one thing: Mom had come for the furniture. I was twelve, watching from the kitchen window as she and her new husband began dismantling what was left of our family home. In the divorce settlement, Dad got the house; Mom got everything inside.[66]

I remember my brother fighting with Mom's new husband over the microwave. My brother won, which felt like a small victory on an otherwise terrible day. Microwaves were new technology then, and keeping that one appliance felt significant.

Recently, Patty and I attended a three-week counseling intensive[67]—something we needed after thirty years of ministry across two continents. During our time there, I wanted to address this memory. As I revisited that day, I noticed something strange. I remembered everything from above, as if I was floating in the upper corner of our kitchen.

"How is that possible?" I asked our counselor.

He explained it was depersonalization—a form of dissociation linked to trauma. It's the mind's protective response to overwhelming stress. My twelve-year-old self, unable to process what was happening, had escaped by viewing it from above.

Reflecting on the memory, anger first rose toward my mom and her husband. How could they be more concerned about furniture than me? Why were they discussing the best way to carry something out the door while ignoring my presence?

Then the anger shifted toward my dad. Where was he that day? Why did he let us stay home to witness our family being dismantled, one chair and end table at a time?[68]

Respect grew for my brother. Despite being younger and smaller than our new stepdad, he fought valiantly for that microwave. Maybe that's why, to this day, I see him as my hero.

Before the retreat, I had been reading Rusty Rustenbach's book on inner-healing prayer.[69] Following his suggestions, I decided to ask God about that day.

In a quiet moment, I asked, "Where were You when this happened?"

Immediately, a picture formed in my mind: my young

self sitting on Jesus's shoulders. That's why I'd been viewing everything from the kitchen corner. I was on His shoulders, watching it all unfold.

Then I asked, "What would You say to my twelve-year-old self?"

Again, the answer came instantly. I saw Jesus look up at me and say, "I'm going to use this for good. It will be good for you and good for others. You'll see."

As I saw myself on His shoulders and heard those words, the memory transformed. The anger dissolved— toward Mom, Dad, and everyone. Even now, thinking of it makes me smile. I wasn't alone. God's intimate presence was near. Satan's interpretation—that I was unloved, forgotten, and abandoned—melted in a moment.

The Shape Of His Spirit

I begin with this story because it demonstrates an essential point: we need a living relationship with God's Spirit. Before Jesus left, He told His disciples, "It is for your good that I am going away. Unless I go away, the Advocate will not come to you; but if I go, I will send him to you" (John 16:7).

Jesus leaving didn't mean Jesus stopped speaking. The Spirit of Christ—the Holy Spirit—is alive and active, speaking to His people today. This is essential as we live on belay with Jesus. It's nearly impossible to live on mission when we're held back by unhealed wounds and lies we believe about ourselves. God's Spirit changes that.

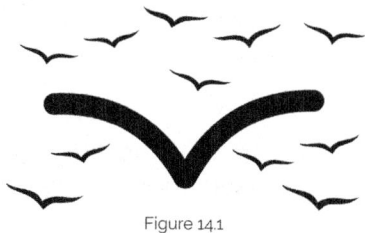
Figure 14.1

Our shape for the Belay Anchor is a simple line drawing of a dove (figure 14.1), representing the Holy Spirit. This image comes from Jesus's baptism:

> As soon as Jesus was baptized, he went up out of the water. At that moment heaven was opened, and he saw the Spirit of God descending like a dove and alighting on him. And a voice from heaven said, "This is my Son, whom I love; with him I am well pleased." (Matthew 3:16–17)

Notice how God's voice spoke when the dove descended, "This is my Son." This passage not only gives us our shape for belaying—a dove—it shows us how to deepen our relationship with God's Spirit: listen for His voice.

Prayer Is Conversation

We say prayer is a conversation with God. But have you noticed that we do all the talking? If it's really a conversation, shouldn't we give Him space to speak?

My favorite Old Testament prophet is Amos. I love his admission of how unremarkable he was.

> I was neither a prophet nor the son of a prophet, but I was a shepherd, and I also took care of sycamore-fig trees. But the Lord took

me from tending the flock and said to me, "Go, prophesy to my people Israel." (Amos 7:14–15)

Amos wasn't a trained minister. He was a regular guy with regular jobs: sheep-tending and fig-harvesting. Yet God spoke to him and basically said, "Take my words and give them to others" (my paraphrase).

Listen to Amos's description of God:

> He who forms the mountains, who creates the wind, and who reveals his thoughts to mankind, who turns dawn to darkness, and treads on the heights of the earth—the Lord God Almighty is his name. (Amos 4:13).

Did you catch that? Amos says God "reveals his thoughts to mankind." This isn't unique to Amos' writing. Throughout Scripture, God is a speaking God:

Daniel declares, "There is a God in heaven who reveals mysteries" (Daniel 2:28).

Isaiah promises personal guidance:

> How gracious he will be when you cry for help! As soon as he hears, he will answer you... Whether you turn to the right or to the left, your ears will hear a voice behind you, saying, "This is the way; walk in it." (Isaiah 30:19–21)

In Jeremiah, God invites us to ask boldly: "Call to me and I will answer you and tell you great and unsearchable things you do not know" (Jeremiah 33:2–3).

Yes, God speaks through Scripture—we'll explore that in a moment. But He also speaks personally and directly to

His people today. Call to Him and He will answer. Ask and expect to hear.

Listening Prayer

Let me introduce something called "listening prayer." Honestly, the term is redundant. Like saying "free gift," "safe haven," or "unexpected surprise," it repeats itself. To pray is to listen.

The prophet Habakkuk understood this. "I will stand at my watch and station myself on the ramparts; I will look to see what he will say to me, and what answer I am to give to this complaint" (Habakkuk 2:1).

Notice his posture—standing, watching, and looking to see what God will say. Habakkuk *expected* God to speak.

I learned this during our counseling intensive. I asked God two simple questions: "Where were You when this happened?" and "What would You say to my twelve-year-old self?" His answers transformed a traumatic memory into a testimony of His intimate presence.

Here are seven practical questions to guide your listening. Find a quiet place, ask one or two at a time, then listen. Journal what word, picture, or impression the Spirit brings:

1. *"Jesus, what do You see when You look at me?"*

    See yourself through God's eyes. Remember: "Jesus looked at him and loved him" (Mark 10:21).

2. *"Is there anything I'm carrying that You want me to*

release?"

> Receive His freedom from your burdens. "Come to me, all who are weary and burdened, and I will give you rest" (Matthew 11:28).

3. *"What are You inviting me into this season?"*

> Open your heart to His direction. "My sheep listen to my voice; I know them, and they follow me" (John 10:27).

4. *"Do You have a word or picture for me in this season?"*

> God often speaks through images and metaphors. "Your word is a lamp to my feet and a light to my path" (Psalm 119:105).

5. *"What brings You joy when You think of me?"*

> Discover His delight in you. "The Lord your God is with you, the Mighty Warrior who saves. He will take great delight in you; in his love he will no longer rebuke you, but will rejoice over you with singing" (Zephaniah 3:17).

6. *"Is anything grieving Your heart right now?"*

> Join Jesus in His compassion. "When he saw the crowds, he had compassion on them, because they were harassed and helpless, like sheep without a shepherd" (Matthew 9:36).

7. *"How do You want me to join You today?"*

> Listen for practical ways to partner with Him right now. "Whatever you did for one of the least of these brothers and sisters of mine, you

did for me" (Matthew 25:40).

I encourage you to revisit these questions during your quiet times.[70] As you practice listening prayer, you'll discover what I learned years ago as a young, financially-stressed youth pastor: God speaks personally through His Spirit and powerfully through His Word.

The Shape Of His Word

When I became a youth pastor in 1997, it was a stretch for everyone. The church had never had a paid youth pastor before, and we weren't sure how to start a family on so little.

Patty and I moved into the church parsonage—no rent to worry about, thankfully, because the church was only able to pay us $400 a month. To make ends meet, we both took part-time jobs. Patty worked at Maurice's clothing store while I answered phones and cleaned hearing aids at an audiology clinic. (Hearing aids? Was God preparing me to learn how to listen?)

Despite our efforts, I stressed about money constantly. Every grocery trip, every gas fill-up, and every unexpected expense heightened my anxiety.

That season, I decided to memorize the entire Sermon on the Mount.[71] It saved me. With Jesus's words committed to memory, they convicted and comforted my anxious heart throughout the day:

> Do not store up for yourselves treasures on earth, where moths and vermin destroy, and where thieves break in and steal. But store up

for yourselves treasures in heaven... For where your treasure is, there your heart will be also. (Matthew 6:19-21)

Therefore I tell you, do not worry about your life, what you will eat or drink; or about your body, what you will wear... Look at the birds of the air; they do not sow or reap or store away in barns, and yet your heavenly Father feeds them. Are you not much more valuable than they? (Matthew 6:25-26)

As these words sank from my head to my heart, something shifted. The worry dissolved. I felt free— genuinely free. My faith felt strong enough to move mountains. And somehow, supernaturally, our finances always stretched to cover our needs.

Saturating myself in God's Word had a powerful effect. It gave me the faith to keep obeying the Father's voice. His Spirit had led us into ministry, and His Word gave us the courage to follow through. This experience taught me that His Spirit and His Word work together.

Remember my counseling intensive? When Jesus showed me I was on His shoulders, I experienced the truth of Scripture: "You saw how the Lord your God carried you, as a father carries his son, all the way you went until you reached this place" (Deuteronomy 1:31).

Now that I'm in my fifties, maybe this passage from Isaiah fits better! "Even to your old age and gray hairs I am he, I am he who will sustain you. I have made you and I will carry you" (Isaiah 46:4).

When Jesus looked up at me and said, "I'm going to use

this for good," I was hearing Romans 8:28 personalized for my twelve-year-old heart: "We know that in all things God works for the good of those who love him."

The Spirit and the Word work together. Jesus promised it would be this way:

> All this I have spoken while still with you. But the Advocate, the Holy Spirit, whom the Father will send in my name, will teach you all things and will remind you of everything I have said to you. (John 14:25-26)

> When he, the Spirit of truth, comes, he will guide you into all the truth. He will not speak on his own; he will speak only what he hears. (John 16:13)

Since His Spirit and His Word work together, they must be in alignment. This is crucial: when we listen for the Spirit's voice, we must ask, "Does this sound like Jesus? Does it align with God's Word?"

The Holy Spirit will never contradict the Holy Bible. He illuminates, personalizes, and brings it to life in our circumstances. In Appendix C, I'll include Scripture declarations you can speak over yourself, aligning your thoughts with God's Word.

Figure 14.2

Therefore, the symbol I introduced above does double duty. It not only reminds us of the Spirit's presence (figure

14.1), but also the open pages of Scripture (figure 14.2).

The Shape Of Being Sent

Actually ... let's make that triple duty. Our symbol for belay is also intended to look like an arrow (figure 14.3). Because both the Spirit and the Word have this message in common: "Go."

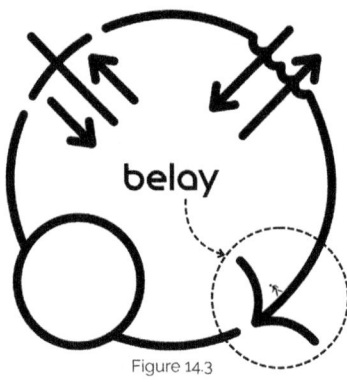

Figure 14.3

When I was a youth pastor, a missionary from Eastern Europe visited our church. His text was Isaiah 49:6:

> It is too small a thing for you to be my servant to restore the tribes of Jacob and bring back those of Israel I have kept. I will also make you a light for the Gentiles, that my salvation may reach to the ends of the earth.

I was blown away. Despite reading the Bible cover to cover several times, I'd somehow missed God's missionary heart in the Old Testament. I thought the "Go into all the world" passages didn't start until the New Testament.

As I've continued reading Scripture, I've discovered something profound: from start to finish, the Bible reveals God as the first and greatest missionary, consistently moving toward people in love. It begins in the garden:

> Then the man and his wife heard the sound of the Lord God as he was walking in the garden in the cool of the day, and they hid from the Lord God among the trees of the garden. But the Lord God called to the man, "Where are you?" (Genesis 3:8–9)

God was pursuing Adam and Eve—the first people—the first sinners. "Where are you?" He asks. This is God on mission, looking for the lost.

Jesus embodies this mission: "For the Son of Man came to seek and to save the lost" (Luke 19:10). The Gospels show Him doing exactly that—pursuing, finding, and saving.

Then Jesus sends His followers to continue: "You will receive power when the Holy Spirit comes on you; and you will be my witnesses in Jerusalem, and in all Judea and Samaria, and to the ends of the earth" (Acts 1:8).

The early church understood the assignment:

Peter wrote,

> Live such good lives among the pagans that, though they accuse you of doing wrong, they may see your good deeds and glorify God on the day he visits us. (1 Peter 2:12)

Paul wrote,

> Be wise in the way you act toward outsiders; make the most of every opportunity. Let your

conversation be always full of grace, seasoned with salt, so that you may know how to answer everyone. (Colossians 4:5–6)

John helps us see the mission's fruit:

> After this I looked, and there before me was a great multitude that no one could count, from every nation, tribe, people and language, standing before the throne and before the Lamb. They were wearing white robes and were holding palm branches in their hands. (Revelation 7:9)

Genesis to Revelation, the Bible isn't about people searching for God—it's about God pursuing people. His mission isn't a subplot; it's the entire narrative.

You On Mission

Likewise, you on belay—you on mission—isn't a side quest. It's the main thing. The Spirit guides, the Word grounds, and both propel us forward into mission.

Having rediscovered the ancient Anchors—Belong, Believe, and Become—for ourselves, we're now equipped to guide others along the Anchored Path, too. This is the shape of belaying.

How do we begin? By creating space at our tables, in our conversations, and with our resources.

Let's begin with the table.

Questions For Reflection

14. THE SHAPE OF BELAYING

1. Two questions (along with God's answers) transformed a traumatic memory: "Where were You?" and "What would You say to me?" Think of a difficult moment from your past. Ask God these questions and listen for His response.

2. Which of the seven listening-prayer questions resonate most right now? Choose one or two this week. Journal the word, picture, or impression you receive.

3. My anxiety dissolved by memorizing Scripture. What worry or fear in your life needs to be addressed by God's Word? Find three Scriptures that speak to it, craft a short declaration from them, and memorize it.

4. Our Belay symbol represents the Spirit, the Word, and being sent. In which area do you feel strongest? Weakest? What specific practice would strengthen your weakest area this month?

5. "Genesis to Revelation, the Bible isn't about people searching for God—it's about God pursuing people." How does this reframe your story? Who is God pursuing through you, and what is one next step you can take?

15. SPACE AT THE TABLE

Jesus replied, "They do not need to go away. You give them something to eat." (Matthew 14:16)

"Where should we eat?" I called back to our college vocal group as I drove our fifteen-passenger van through Milwaukee, Wisconsin.

Our director had made me the team leader, which somehow meant I did most of the driving. Hours on the road, music playing, conversations and laughter drifting from the back seats. I think we enjoyed our travel days more than our performances.

But this particular moment wasn't that enjoyable. As my question bounced around the van, I got the predictable chaos of responses. "Subway!" came from one of the girls. "McDonald's!" shouted one of the guys. "Pizza Hut!" "Denny's!" Each suggestion louder than the last, as if volume might sway my decision.

Someone had to choose. If we were going to eat—and we definitely needed to eat—I had to pick the table where we'd gather. I pulled into a Popeye's. Not a single soul had suggested it, but hey, I was driving.

Looking back, maybe it was good preparation for fatherhood. Now, Patty and I have four grown kids, but we still remember how the "where should we eat" question generated just as many opinions. Sometimes you have to make the call before your crew devolves into a pack of hangry animals.

That van full of hungry classmates taught me something about living on belay—we have a decision to make about tables. Not just where to grab a quick meal on a road trip, but something more significant: understanding which tables we're called to gather around and why.

As we explore being on belay—living purposefully and on mission with Jesus—we need to consider three essential tables: His table, your table, and their table.

His Table

In chapter 6, we saw how Jesus chose the most ordinary act to help us remember Him. Just before going to the cross, He shared a meal with His disciples.

> When the hour came, Jesus and his apostles reclined at the table. And he took bread, gave thanks and broke it, and gave it to them, saying, "This is my body given for you; do this in remembrance of me."
>
> In the same way, after the supper he took the

cup, saying, "This cup is the new covenant in my blood, which is poured out for you." (Luke 22:14, 19–20)

Jesus could have chosen any symbol, ritual, or grand gesture to be remembered by. Instead, he picked something we do every day—eating together. If I may paraphrase a bit, Jesus essentially says: "Remember me every time you sit down to eat."

"Every time bread touches your lips, remember my body, broken for you. My brokenness makes you whole."

"Every time a cup touches your lips, remember my blood, poured out for you. This is the cost of forgiveness."

This table is the central reminder of Jesus's work —handed down through generations since that first reimagined Passover when He transformed an ancient meal into something new.

That's why Paul writes:

> For I received from the Lord what I also passed on to you: The Lord Jesus, on the night he was betrayed, took bread, and when he had given thanks, he broke it and said, "This is my body, which is for you; do this in remembrance of me."
>
> In the same way, after supper he took the cup, saying, "This cup is the new covenant in my blood; do this, whenever you drink it, in remembrance of me."
>
> For whenever you eat this bread and drink this cup, you proclaim the Lord's death until he comes. (1 Corinthians 11:23–26)

Notice something striking here. Paul says we "proclaim the Lord's death until he comes." Not His life. Not His teachings. Not His miracles. His death.

Why?

Paul understood something we might forget: there's no Sunday morning celebration without Friday evening devastation. The empty tomb only matters because of the bloodied cross.

Christianity isn't about self-improvement. It's not a program for becoming a better version of yourself. It's about agreeing with God that we are so helpless, so broken, so far gone that God Himself had to physically show up in the person of Jesus.

If Paul had simply said we proclaim the Lord's life until He comes, it would have sounded nice—inspirational even. But it would have left out the crucial part: Jesus set the table with His own body and blood.

So here's my question: Are you eating at His table? Let me put it more directly. Do you agree with God that without Him, you're a broken sinner heading for judgment and hell? Do you believe that He alone can transform you into a forgiven saint?

This is what it means to eat at His table. It's not about bringing something to offer. It's about coming empty-handed and hungry. It's about receiving His gift of mercy and forgiveness—the same way a starving person receives a life-giving meal.

Jesus expresses it this way:

> Very truly I tell you, the one who believes has eternal life. I am the bread of life. Your ancestors ate the manna in the wilderness, yet they died. But here is the bread that comes down from heaven, which anyone may eat and not die. I am the living bread that came down from heaven. Whoever eats this bread will live forever. This bread is my flesh, which I will give for the life of the world. (John 6:47–51)

Jesus doesn't ask us to cook the meal. Nor does He ask us to set the table. He simply invites us to eat—to receive what He's already prepared.

Living on belay begins here, not with what we do for God, but with receiving what He's already done for us. We can't truly belay others—we can't guide them along the Anchored Path—until we're first secured to the Rock ourselves.

That security comes from one place: His table. Where broken bread reminds us we can be made whole, and the cup reminds us we can be forgiven.

Come to His table. There's always room for one more.

Your Table

In Chapter 6, we learned three ways the New Testament authors complete the sentence: "The Son of Man came …"

> "… to give his life as a ransom for many." (Mark 10:45)
> "… to seek and to save the lost." (Luke 19:10)
> "… eating and drinking." (Luke 7:34)

The first two describe Jesus's purpose: to give His life and save the lost. The third describes His method: eating and drinking.

Look through the Gospels and you'll notice something striking. Many of Jesus's most pivotal ministry moments happened around tables. It's how He communicated the first Anchor: you Belong.

His first miracle? The wedding at Cana, where He turned water to wine. Not to show off His power, but to keep the party going—to keep people gathered around the tables (John 2).

His announcement of leaving? The Last Supper (Matthew 26).

His post-resurrection appearance? Cooking breakfast on the beach for guilt-ridden Peter (John 21).

Even eternity begins with a meal—the Wedding Supper of the Lamb (Revelation 19).

If significant ministry moments happened around tables for Jesus, shouldn't we expect the same? Shouldn't our tables also be a place where we communicate to our guests, "You belong"?

A family therapist, Anne Fishel, said in an interview:

> I sort of half-joke that I could be out of business if more families had regular family dinners, because so many of the things that I try to do in family therapy actually get accomplished by regular dinners.[72]

She went on to say that regular family dinners are

linked to lower rates of depression, anxiety, substance abuse, eating disorders, tobacco use, and early teenage pregnancy. They are also linked to higher resilience and self-esteem.

I doubt this just applies to biological families. What if we open our tables to neighbors, friends, and strangers? Why shouldn't we see the same transformation?

I can already hear the pushback: "I can't afford to host people. It's expensive." You know what? This is an ancient objection! When Jesus was teaching a massive crowd, his disciples came to him with the same concern. Take a look at what they said:

> This is a remote place ... and it's already very late. Send the people away so they can go to the surrounding countryside and villages and buy themselves something to eat. (Mark 6:35-36)

In other words: "Jesus, we can't afford to feed all these people. It's too expensive. Send them away to handle it themselves."

But Jesus gave them a surprising response: "You give them something to eat" (Mark 6:37).

The disciples were incredulous. "That would take more than half a year's wages! Are we to go and spend that much on bread and give it to them to eat?" (Mark 6:37).

Then Jesus asked a simple question: "How many loaves do you have? Go and see." (Mark 6:38).

Five loaves and two fish. Barely enough for one family, let alone five thousand. But when they placed that meager lunch in Jesus's hands, he blessed it, broke it, and gave it to the disciples to distribute. Everyone ate until they were full, and they collected twelve baskets of leftovers.[73]

When we partner with God in sharing our table, I believe he shows up and provides. Let me tell you about a previous Easter Sunday.

Patty had prepared dinner for our family and a couple of friends. Then, in typical Patty fashion, she started inviting everyone she saw: the neighbor walking their dog, a few people from church, the single mom who needed a break ...[74]

I panicked internally. We didn't have enough food. Eight portions don't feed sixteen. But somehow—and I can't explain it—we fed everyone and had leftovers for the week. Every time I opened the fridge and saw those containers, and reheated another portion, I thought, "This shouldn't exist. There shouldn't have been enough." But God multiplies what we offer.

The ancient Greek philosopher Epicurus understood something profound about tables: "We should look for someone to eat and drink with before looking for something to eat and drink."[75]

How often do we do that? Why don't we recognize that company matters more than cuisine? That the relationship matters more than the recipe?

Even our language remembers! The word "companion" comes from Latin—*com* means "with" and *panis* means "bread." A companion is literally someone you share bread with!

Your table becomes a place for companionship and

belonging. Conversations flow. Barriers come down. The kingdom of God shows up between salad and dessert.

As Michael Frost writes in his book *Surprise the World!*:

> The table is a great equalizer in relationships. When we eat together we discover the inherent humanity of all people. We share stories. And hopes. And fears. And disappointments. People open up to each other. And we ourselves can open up to share the same things—including our faith in Jesus.[76]

Ask yourself this question: Who needs to sit at my table this week?

Their Table

Living on belay also means praying for opportunities to be guests at other tables. The most powerful ministry can happen when we accept an invitation rather than extend one, when we let others serve us and receive their hospitality.

We've established that Jesus did a lot of ministry around tables. But here's something you might have missed: it didn't happen at *His* table. Know why? He didn't have one!

"Foxes have dens and birds have nests," Jesus said, "but the Son of Man has no place to lay his head" (Luke 9:58). No home meant no dining room. No dining room meant no table of His own.

So, when we see Jesus sharing a meal, it was always at someone else's table. Look at where He ate:

At Zacchaeus's house, the hated tax collector (Luke 19:5). At Matthew's house, surrounded by "sinners" (Matthew 9:10). At a Pharisee's house, where a sinful woman washed His feet (Luke 7:36).

Do you know what this says to me?

Yes, it's good to be hospitable and share our table. But honestly? That's pretty safe. Our table is our turf. We control what's served, when it's served, and maybe to some degree, what gets talked about. It's still good—don't get me wrong—but it's comfortable.

Their table? That's where things get interesting.

César Chávez said it best: "If you really want to make a friend, go to someone's house and eat with him ... the people who give you their food give you their heart."[77]

A few months ago, I experienced this firsthand. Zhou, a friend of mine who's also a Chinese immigrant, texted me out of the blue: "Can you come to my house for hot pot?"

We drove forty minutes to his home. Shortly after arriving, while we took off our shoes and hung our coats, Zhou said something unexpected: "My mom's friends prayed for her when she had meningitis, and she was healed immediately. Please let me introduce you to her."

Before I could even process that, he continued: "As a result, my mom wants to become a Christian now and study the Bible. Can you help her?"

My jaw dropped. Here was Zhou—who'd told me multiple times he's an atheist—asking me to help his mother follow Jesus.

"Of course," I said, still a bit stunned. We connected his mom with another Chinese woman from our church who could teach her in Mandarin.

Then Zhou said something that still makes me smile: "Also, if my mom wants a ride to church, I'll be happy to drive her there."

An atheist son driving his mother to church. How did that happen? It didn't happen at my table; it happened at his. Walls came down, and his heart opened up.

And here's the thing: their table doesn't necessarily mean their home. It can just mean going where your neighbors already gather:

Coffee shops where regulars solve the world's problems. Breweries where coworkers unwind after a long week. Backyard BBQs where the entire neighborhood shows up.

In the church I grew up in, it was somewhat taboo to eat and drink where the "sinners" did. While the people of that group were wonderful and godly ... they may have been just a bit legalistic, too. So, while the "sinners" had a pig roast at the fairgrounds, we had our potluck in the church basement. Safe, separate (and a tad sanctimonious).

But Jesus, by His own example, pushes us out. He calls us to be guests at *their* tables. Guess what happens when we do? He shows up, right there with us.

Psalm 23 takes on new meaning: "You prepare a table before me in the presence of my enemies." Not in the safety of the church basement, or the comfort of our dining room. But right there, amidst those who might oppose us—but become friends if we'd just sit down at their table.

Space At The Table

To help you remember this simple practice of sharing meals, I want you to picture the circle of belonging from the first section of this book (figure 6.1)—but now with a few place settings in it (figure 15.1). The circle that stands for God's love becomes a table where belonging happens.

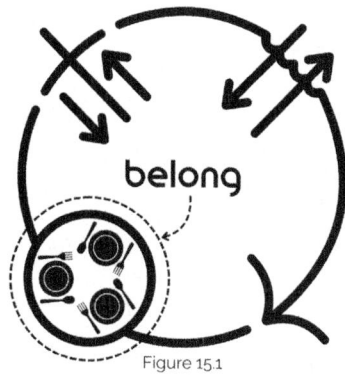
Figure 15.1

The Son of Man came to seek and save the lost—and He did it by eating and drinking with people. They even criticized Him for it: "Here is a glutton and a drunkard, a friend of tax collectors and sinners" (Luke 7:34).

But Jesus knew something we may not realize: Tables are holy ground. Meals are ministry. Breaking bread breaks down barriers.

Consider the shift Jesus brought. Old Testament thinking said, "Don't touch the leper—he'll make you unclean" (Leviticus 5:3). New Testament thinking says, "Let me touch the leper so I can make him clean" (Matthew 8:2-3).

The same principle applies to tables. Old thinking says, "Don't eat with them—they might contaminate you." New thinking says, "Let's share a meal—transformation happens at tables."

When you carry the Spirit of God, every place becomes holy ground. Every table—His, yours, and theirs—becomes an opportunity to communicate to others, "you belong."

So, here's the question to help us be the "Belong Anchor" for others on the Anchored Path: How will you make room at the table this week?

> Will you come empty-handed to His table, receiving only what He can give?
>
> Will you open your table, trusting God to multiply what you offer?
>
> Will you accept an invitation to their table, going where Jesus would go?

The van full of college students taught me that someone has to choose where we eat. But following Jesus taught me something more important. It's not just about choosing where to eat—it's also about choosing who to eat with.

Sometimes, the most important choice is simply showing up with an empty chair beside us and a readiness to share a meal.

Questions For Reflection

1. Consider your relationship with "His table." Are you trying to earn God's love instead of receiving it? What would it look like to approach communion—and daily life—as someone truly hungry for what only Jesus can provide?

2. Consider your own table. Who could you invite to your table this week? What fears or practical concerns hold you back, and how might God be inviting you to trust Him to multiply what you have?

3. Where are "their tables" in your community—the natural places your neighbors eat and drink? How could you become a regular presence there without an agenda, simply available for whatever God might do?

4. Jesus's ministry often happened around meals. Can you recall a time when a shared meal led to a significant spiritual conversation or breakthrough? How might viewing meals as ministry reshape your weekly routine?

5. When you carry the Spirit of God, every place becomes holy ground. What tables or spaces is He calling you to enter, trusting His presence in you to make them holy?

16. SPACE IN OUR CONVERSATIONS

Let your conversation be always full of grace, seasoned with salt, so that you may know how to answer everyone. (Colossians 4:6)

Patty came home from the local rec center, breathless and excited. "Bob says they're desperate for bus drivers. I think I might apply. They'll even give me a thousand-dollar sign-on bonus."

Bob, her instructor, has this gift for making whatever he's doing sound like the best thing in the world. His classes are packed each week. Families are delighted when they find out he's their child's bus driver. And apparently, he can make driving a school bus sound like an adventure worth having. (Turns out, it is!)

I thought about it for a moment, then said to Patty, "You and I both know that I'm the one who loves driving. I think I should apply."

So I did. Three months later, Bob and I both had thousand-dollar bonuses in our bank accounts—him for recruiting and me for signing on—and those dollars were burning holes in our pockets. One early morning during our daily bus pre-check, Bob gave me a fist pump, and declared, "We need to celebrate!"

Our celebration was a simple meal at our house, around our table, talking for hours. We started with bus stories—the perils of mountain driving, the kid who nearly burned the bus down, and the daily drama at the depot. Then somehow we were talking about Boulder's history, about Patty's knee surgery, and about moving to Boulder. Then, as naturally as breathing, we found ourselves talking about dreams, hopes, and what matters most.

As I helped clear the plates, I marveled at how our conversation had naturally deepened throughout the evening. It reminded me of those colorblind glasses I told you about in Chapter 13.

Just as my glasses revealed colors that had always been present but invisible to me, I suddenly saw something that had always been true about conversations: they move through distinct colors, each one representing a different level of connection.

I know that might sound strange. But stick with me.

Space To Believe

If creating space at our tables makes room for people to belong (like we explored in the last chapter), then creating space in our conversations makes room for them to believe.

Jesus knew this. On a dusty road from Jerusalem to Emmaus, He demonstrated exactly how to move through the conversational colors—green, red, blue, white—with two heartbroken disciples, each color drawing those disciples deeper into truth.

To help you visualize this, I'd like you to imagine a speech bubble surrounding the cross of the Believe Anchor (figure 16.1).

Figure 16.1

As we zoom into the bubble (figure 16.2), we can see the four colors—four types of conversation—that help us guide others in discovering Jesus's invitation to believe.

Let's dig into this.

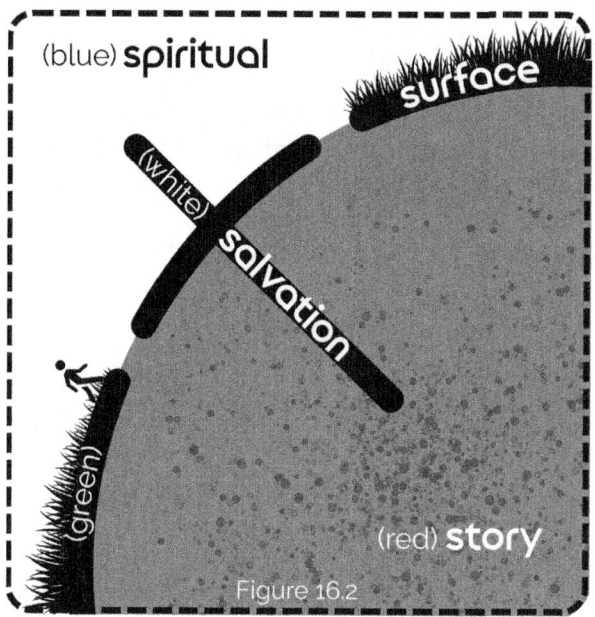

Figure 16.2

Green: Surface Conversation

After the crucifixion, the disciples scattered. None of them were prepared for Jesus's death on the cross—and even less prepared for the resurrection. When He did rise, most found it hard to believe.

When Jesus came upon two disciples walking to Emmaus (Luke 24:13-35), He kept His identity hidden. (I'd love to know how He did that!) Rather than startle or shock them, He walked alongside them and asked, "What are you discussing together as you walk along?" (Luke 24:17).

That's it. No confrontational "If you died today, would you go to heaven or hell?"[78] No heavy theological opener. Just "Hey guys, what's up? What are you talking about?"

The other day, Patty had the "Sirens" over for lunch.

These are her swimming buddies from the rec center. A dozen or so women and two older men filled our living room with chatter. I found myself in a surface conversation with Peter, learning he's been scuba diving all over the world.

Here's the thing: I know nothing about scuba diving, and I'm not even sure I'd like to try it. Snorkeling? Sure. Scuba diving? Maybe not for me. I'd rather skydive than go that deep below the ocean's surface. But that's the beauty of a surface conversation. My priority isn't me and my preferences. The person I'm talking with is the priority. And if I'm ignorant of the topic, I get to learn and ask questions!

So I asked Peter: Where have you dived? How long did you train? Do you ever get nervous down there? Peter lit up. For twenty minutes, I heard about coral reefs in Belize and night dives in Hawaii. I didn't need expertise or experience. I just needed curiosity.

When you view Earth from space, what color dominates the continents? Green, right? It covers the surface as trees, grass, plants—and we need all that oxygen-producing green to breathe.

Surface conversations work the same way—they give oxygen to conversation and relationships. They create an environment for deeper connection to grow because people feel valued and seen when we ask about their lives. Showing interest is the same as showing love, and all you need to do is ask questions.

Consider the story of Creation in Genesis. Before God created people on Day Six, He spent five days preparing the surface—light, sky, land, sea, plants, and stars. The stage had to be set before His beloved—Adam and Eve—were created.

Surface conversations aren't time-wasters; they're trust-builders. Jesus Himself often started with the ordinary before moving to the eternal:

> "Got any fish?" (John 21:5)
> "Will you give me a drink?" (John 4:7)
> "What are you discussing?" (Luke 24:17)

As someone on belay with Jesus, I take this as permission to spend time preparing the surface. Learning names. Being friendly. Showing genuine interest. Because sometimes the most spiritual thing you can do is ask someone about scuba diving.

Try these surface conversation starters:

> *What's your name?"* ("A person's name is to that person the sweetest and most important sound in any language.")[79]
>
> "What's been the highlight of your week so far?"
>
> What do you like to do when you're not at [work/school]?"
>
> "What's your favorite thing about living in (place name)?"

Watch how people come alive when someone shows genuine curiosity in their life.

Red: Story Conversation

With all the pines in Colorado, one could argue that the most predominant color in the state is green. And I agree, there's a lot of it. But, do you know what you find at the base of those trees? Red. Red rock and red dirt. As mentioned in Chapter 13, the word "Colorado" literally means "color red."

Going below the surface—whether it's skin or soil—you encounter the same color: red. When we fight our fear of going below the surface in conversation, we discover red conversation: a person's story.

At the surface, we know names and interesting facts about people—which is important. But a story conversation helps us hear what's important to them—their hopes, dreams, fears, struggles, and aspirations.

Kenny was a pastor of another international church in Asia. He seemed to be at odds with other pastors in his city, and sadly, many just wrote him off. I knew there had to be more, so I invited him to coffee. As we sat down, I said, "Kenny, would you tell me your story? I want to understand."

Kenny poured out his heart for more than an hour. The ups and downs of leading a church among expats. The struggle of raising a family in a foreign culture. His hopes and dreams for the future. Kenny and I became friends—simply because I was willing to hear his story and not write him off. Six years later, when our family left China, Kenny pulled me aside to let me know how much my "tell me your story" question had meant to him.

Story conversations reveal the "why" behind the "what." They transform acquaintances into friends, and friends into family.

Jesus models this willingness to hear people's stories on the road to Emmaus. After His opening "What are you discussing" question, the disciples are shocked. They're stunned that this stranger doesn't know about recent events. "Are you the only one visiting Jerusalem who does not know the things that have happened there in these days?" (Luke 24:18).

Their reaction reminds me of my kids' reaction when I don't know the latest internet meme that they've known about for weeks!

So Jesus asks another simple question: "What things?" (Luke 24:19). That's it. Two words. And those two words release a flood:

> "About Jesus of Nazareth," they replied. "He was a prophet, powerful in word and deed before God and all the people. The chief priests and our rulers handed him over to be sentenced to death, and they crucified him; but we had hoped that he was the one who was going to redeem Israel." (Luke 24:19-21)

Did you catch their heartbreaking phrase? "We had hoped."

With just the question, "What things?" Jesus moved the conversation from surface to story. From facts to feelings. From information to heartbreak. I wonder how many people are one question away from sharing their real hopes and fears—if we'll just be loving and patient enough to ask, and brave enough to actually listen.

Jesus asked over 300 questions in the four Gospels. Look at just a few:

> "What do you want me to do?" (Mark 10:36)
> "Who do you say I am?" (Luke 9:20)
> "What is it you want?" (Matthew 20:21)
> "What do you think?" (Matthew 18:12)
> "Why are you so afraid?" (Mark 4:40)

Notice two things: First, Jesus didn't ask combative questions like "Says who?" or "Can you prove it?" Second, He rarely asked yes or no questions. Instead, He asked thought-provoking questions that took people below the surface and into their precious stories.

You can do the same thing. Consider trying one or more of these story conversation prompts:

> *"Tell me more about that."*
>
> *"How did that affect you?"*
>
> *"What would you like to be true about your life in ten years?"*
>
> *"What's something you've always hoped for?"*
>
> *"Would you tell me your story? I want to understand."*

Watch how the conversation shifts from green to red, facts to feelings, and surface to story.

Blue: Spiritual Conversation

Once we've moved through green (surface) and red (story), we naturally arrive at blue—the spiritual

16. SPACE IN OUR CONVERSATIONS

dimension that's been there all along, waiting to be acknowledged.

No matter where you are, imagine yourself walking outside and looking up. What color dominates? Not green or red—those are below your feet. It's blue—sky blue.

Blue stretches above us, vast and ever-present. Yet we rarely notice it because when we're walking, biking, or driving, we don't look up—we have to look ahead.

The spiritual realm is like our blue sky. More of life is spiritual than we realize, but we rarely notice because our minds stay focused on what's right in front of us.

Jacob of the Old Testament discovered this truth. After encountering God in a dream, he woke up stunned: "Surely the LORD is in this place, and I was not aware of it" (Genesis 28:16).

The writer of Hebrews echoes this reality, "Do not forget to show hospitality to strangers, for by so doing some people have shown hospitality to angels without knowing it" (Hebrews 13:2).

The presence of God. The reality of angels. The nearness of the spiritual realm is as close as our skin, but we're often unaware. As you allow God's Spirit to awaken spiritual reality in you, He can use you to awaken that reality in others.

Watch how naturally the disciples' conversation with Jesus turns spiritual:

> In addition, some of our women amazed us. They went to the tomb early this morning but didn't find his body. They came and told us that

they had seen a vision of angels, who said he was alive. Then some of our companions went to the tomb and found it just as the women had said, but they did not see Jesus (Luke 24:22-24).

The resurrection, visions, angels. This spiritual conversation is still flowing from Jesus's two-word question: "What things?"

No awkward transition. No forced religious agenda. Just natural progression from green to red to blue—from surface to story to spiritual. The disciples brought it up themselves because Jesus had created space for them to process what was really on their hearts.

Here's what I've learned about blue conversations:

First, we need to drop our "church filter." We often talk one way at church and another way everywhere else. What if we talked as if believing in God and the supernatural was just normal?

The night that my bus-driving buddy Bob came over, he ended the evening by telling us about a wild dream he'd had the night before. Even though I knew Bob wasn't a Jesus-follower yet, I said, "It seems like God might be talking to you through your dream. Would you mind if I prayed about it, and then shared my thoughts with you?" He gladly agreed. After taking a day or so to pray, I emailed him what I believed God might be saying. About a week later, Bob sent a text expressing how grateful and moved he was by my interpretation. He was especially grateful for the scriptures I'd shared in the email.

Second, offer to pray. When someone shares a struggle or hope, simply ask: "Would it be okay if I spoke a blessing over that?" or "Can I pray for you about that?" It's unusual for someone to turn down such an offer.

Here are a few questions to bridge a conversation from story to spiritual:

> *"How can I pray for you this week?"*
>
> *"Have you ever experienced something you couldn't explain?"*
>
> *"What role does faith play in your life?"*
>
> *"I've been thinking about [spiritual topic]—what's your take on that?"*
>
> *"What do you think God might be trying to say through this?"*

The sky is blue and always has been. With God's help, you can help someone say, "Surely the LORD is in this place, and I was not aware of it."

White: Salvation Conversation

Jesus says to His followers, "You are the light of the world" (Matthew 5:14). The conversations we've been talking about in this chapter are ways of letting our light shine.

When I was in fourth-grade science class, Mrs. Jacobson showed us something that felt like magic: shine green, red, and blue lights on the same spot, and they combine to create pure white light.

That's exactly what happens in our conversations. When we faithfully move through green surface, red story, and blue spiritual, God often creates space for bright white *salvation* conversations.

If you recall, the two disciples on the road to Emmaus still don't know they're talking to Jesus. Watch how Jesus takes the conversation from spiritual to salvation by talking about the Messiah (Himself):

> He said to them, "How foolish you are, and how slow to believe all that the prophets have spoken! Did not the Messiah have to suffer these things and then enter his glory?" And beginning with Moses and all the Prophets, he explained to them what was said in all the Scriptures concerning himself. (Luke 24:25-27)

Notice something remarkable—they didn't get offended, even though He called them foolish! Rather than feeling put off, they begged Jesus to stay:

> But they urged him strongly, "Stay with us, for it is nearly evening; the day is almost over."
>
> So he went in to stay with them. When he was at the table with them, he took bread, gave thanks, broke it and began to give it to them. Then their eyes were opened and they recognized him...
>
> They asked each other, "Were not our hearts burning within us while he talked with us on the road and opened the Scriptures to us?" (Luke 24:29-32)

Their hearts were burning. That's what we pray happens as conversation moves from spiritual to salvation, and we share about the good news of Jesus.

16. SPACE IN OUR CONVERSATIONS

Remember Shan from Chapter 7? He got stuck on creation versus evolution. I could have debated science and Genesis for hours. Instead, I said, "Let's put that aside for now. The most important thing you need to think about is this—what are you going to do with Jesus?"

This is salvation conversation, not a theological debate. While there's certainly a place for apologetics—answering honest questions and removing intellectual barriers—salvation conversations are more pointed. They move past arguments to the heart of the matter, leading to the essential question: Who is Jesus, and what will you do with Him?

Jesus Himself made it this direct with His friend Martha: "I am the resurrection and the life. The one who believes in me will live, even though they die... Do you believe this?" (John 11:25-26).

"Yes, Lord, I believe that you are the Messiah" (John 11:27).

That's the moment—when someone sees Jesus for who He really is. Try these salvation conversation transitions:

> "Can I share what Jesus has meant in my life?"
>
> "What do you think about Jesus?"
>
> "Would you like to know more about following Jesus?"
>
> "Can I share four spiritual truths that helped me understand what it means to be a Christian?"
>
> "Can I tell you why I believe Jesus is different?"

Remember, you've already built trust through green

surface conversations. You've heard their story—maybe with a passion that made you both see red. You've acknowledged spiritual reality, as encompassing as a bright blue sky.

Now, as His Spirit leads, you can naturally introduce them to the One who brings all the colors together.

The Speed Of Light

For the disciples on the road to Emmaus, their hearts burned because Jesus had patiently walked them through every color. He could have revealed Himself immediately, but instead, He demonstrated that transformation often happens through patient, purposeful conversation. It's not about forcing an agenda or rushing to a "white light" moment. It's about being faithful with each color God gives:

> Showing genuine interest in their interests,
> Listening to hopes and heartaches,
> Acknowledging the spiritual reality around us,
> Introducing people to Jesus.

For the Chinese nursing home gentleman I shared about in chapter 13—after being instantly healed of eleven years of dizziness—he was ready for the light! After telling him, "It wasn't my words—it's who I was talking to," the two of us sat together over lunch.

With tears running down his face, he whispered, "I'm just an old man everyone has forgotten. No one knows I even exist. Why would Jesus heal me?"

My Mandarin was limited then, but I had memorized John

3:16 in Chinese. I said to him:

> 神爱世人，甚至将他的独生子赐给他们，叫一切信他的，不致灭亡，反得永生 (For God so loved the world that he gave his one and only Son, that whoever believes in him shall not perish but have eternal life).

After quoting it, I gave a simple explanation, and then asked, "Will you believe in Jesus?" I think he was almost offended by the question!

He smiled and said, "Of course I believe in Jesus—He just healed me, didn't He?"

Encounters like this remind me that the journey from green to red to blue to white can take years for some, and only minutes for others.

Space In Our Conversations

In the previous chapter, we were challenged to create space at our tables—to make room for people to belong. Here we've discovered that what happens at those tables matters just as much: conversations that help people move from belonging to believing.

> Will you create space in your conversations for God to move?
>
> Will you have the patience to let conversations develop naturally through their colors?
>
> Will you trust that as you're faithful with green, red, and blue, God will create opportunities for white?

I encourage you to sit with these questions before moving to the next chapter, where we'll explore the cost of helping others move from the Anchor of Believing to the Anchor of Becoming.

Questions For Reflection

1. Which color do most of your recent conversations stay in—and what's the main barrier keeping you from moving into the others?

2. Recall a time when someone showed genuine curiosity about your life. How did it affect you? Identify one person who needs that same gift. What will you ask them this week?

3. The disciples shared their heartbreak: "We had hoped." What hopes or disappointments are you carrying? Who creates safe space for you to share your real story?

4. "Were not our hearts burning within us?" When have you felt that in a spiritual conversation? What made that moment different? How could you invite more of it?

5. Showing interest is showing love. Who might be one good question away from sharing their real story—and will you be brave enough to ask, listen, and (if welcomed) offer to pray?

17. SPACE WITH OUR RESOURCES

> *"Which of these three do you think was a neighbor to the man who fell into the hands of robbers?" The expert in the law replied, "The one who had mercy on him." Jesus told him, "Go and do likewise." (Luke 10:36–37)*

It was 1980. The smell of sawdust and window caulk filled the air as Commander Jake handed me a plywood piece cut in the shape of a Bible. Around me, the other Ranger boys clutched their own wooden Bible cutouts, eyes wide as we stood among towering sheets of plate glass that could probably shatter if we weren't careful.

"Remember boys, don't touch the glass," Commander Jake said. He'd brought our entire Royal Rangers group—a ministry for boys that usually met in our church basement—into his glass shop across from the fairgrounds. His company installed and repaired windows for our small Montana town of 3,000, and here we were, a dozen elementary-aged boys surrounded by his fragile inventory.

But we weren't there to work with glass. Commander Jake had spent his own money on plywood and his own time cutting out these Bible shapes that would become Christmas gifts for our parents.

Now he watched as we wrote our favorite verses on paper, then helped us burn the edges for an antique feel (yes, we played with fire that night, too!) We glued the paper to the wood and coated everything with a glossy finish.

That Wednesday evening in his shop has stayed with me for over forty years.

In contrast, dozens of other Wednesday nights in the church basement have faded into a pleasant blur. Why? Because our commander didn't just teach us about walking with Jesus—he showed us. He opened up his workplace, his schedule, and his heart. He let us see him not just as "Ranger Jake" but as "Businessman Jake"—a man who chose to use his resources for the kingdom.

In Chapter 3, we explored a sub-point in the parable of the Good Samaritan[80]—how we're the beaten traveler on the roadside, unconscious to God's love. But there's also the primary point to that story. After the parable, Jesus looks at His audience and says, "Go and do likewise." Be the one who stops. Be the one who sacrifices.

But what does "go and do likewise" actually look like in our daily lives? What resources do we need to invest?

Space To Become

In the last two chapters, we've seen how sharing a meal

can help someone feel they *belong* (Chapter 15) and how an intentional conversation can lead them to *believe* (Chapter 16).

But helping someone *become* more like Christ—that's going to cost us more. Not just a shared meal or a single conversation—it's going to cost the kind of resources the Good Samaritan willingly gave on the dangerous road to Jericho.

To help you understand the resources needed for transformation, imagine a circle with six segments surrounding our Become Anchor (figure 17.1).

Figure 17.1

Each segment represents a resource we see in the Good Samaritan's actions—six investments that (because this pastor can't help but alliterate) all begin with the letter T:

Testimony

When my family moved to China in 2008, it felt like stepping into a parallel universe where everything familiar had been reimagined. From receiving boiling water at restaurants instead of ice water, to seeing women carry umbrellas on sunny days, every detail reminded us we were far from the Midwest.

But beyond these surface differences, we discovered something profound. The story and testimony of the Good Samaritan—so woven into Western consciousness that we name laws after it—was largely unknown in Chinese culture.

This hit home when friends told us about Peng Yu, a young man who'd helped an elderly woman after she fell. She later sued him, claiming he'd caused her fall. The court ordered him to pay her medical expenses, sparking nationwide debate about whether helping strangers was worth the risk.[81] Without cultural stories like the Good Samaritan that celebrate compassion, people naturally protected themselves first.

This isn't about one culture being superior to another—every culture has blind spots. But it revealed to me the transformative power of testimony. The testimony of the Good Samaritan—told and retold for two millennia, has prompted people to build hospitals, adopt orphans, and redefine who counts as their neighbor. It's even shaped legal systems to protect those who stop to help.

This is the power of your testimony too. When you share how God met you in your brokenness, forgave you of your sin, and transformed your life into something new—you invite others to share the same hope as you.

Throughout this book, I've shared pieces of *my* story, hoping that my testimony might help you trust God more deeply. And I pray *your* testimony will encourage others to trust Him as well.

When sharing your story, you might try weaving in phrases like these:

> "God helped me, and I know he can help you."
>
> "I've struggled with the same thing; I know how you feel."
>
> "There's a verse that changed my life; can I share it with you?"

Shortly before we left China in 2019, something had shifted: China instituted national Good Samaritan protections.[82] One could argue many factors led to this change, but I can't help but think that stories—testimonies of compassion—played their part.

What is your story—your testimony—of God's work in your life? What steps can you take to best prepare yourself to share that story with others?

Temperature

Notice this crucial phrase in the Good Samaritan story: "When he saw him, he took pity on him" (Luke 10:33).

That English phrase "took pity" barely scratches the surface of the Greek word Luke uses: σπλάγχνον (splanchnon). The literal meaning is "inner parts" or "bowels." It's everything on your inside—intestines, liver, spleen, etc.

In English, we might say "my heart goes out to someone." The ancient Greeks would say "my guts went out to them." This wasn't polite sympathy on the Good Samaritan's part. It was physical, visceral compassion that arose from the core of his being.

This tells me something. If we're going to belay others in their journey of becoming like Christ, we need to feel their story in our gut. Our hearts can't remain at room temperature.

Think about the theme songs that defined different generations—each one centered on the warmth of genuine friendship. My kids' generation listened to a toy cowboy croon, "You've got a friend in me."[83] The kids in my youth group connected to a group of friends who sang, "I'll be there for you."[84] When I was a teen, I watched a group of chums in a Boston bar celebrate the place, "where everybody knows your name."[85]

Every generation craves the same thing: warm, authentic relationships. The genuine warmth of other Christians likely drew you to Christ. It's my contention that your warmth will do the same for others.

Jesus told the Good Samaritan story precisely because the religious expert He was talking to had a cold heart. The man could quote "love your neighbor as yourself" perfectly (Luke 10:27), but he didn't *feel* it in his gut. His theology was flawless; his temperature was cold.

Jesus tells this story to raise the temperature of *our* hearts, too.

On the Anchored Path of becoming like Christ, the people we serve will stumble (just like we do). They'll disappoint you and themselves. Just when you think they're doing fine, you'll find them beaten up on the side of the road—maybe from their own choices, maybe from circumstances beyond their control.

In those moments, they don't need a cold lecture about where they went wrong. They need someone whose guts wrench at their pain, whose inner parts move with compassion. They need someone willing to feel the weight of their story.

Will you let your temperature rise? Will you let your "guts" go out to them? This visceral compassion —this raised temperature—creates the warmth where transformation can happen.

Talent

In 2005, I took a mission team from our church to Honduras. Among them was Fritz, an old North Dakota farmer who'd never left the state. He saw everything through the lens of his farm life—and initially, that lens wasn't kind.

As our bus wound through the poverty outside Tegucigalpa, heading to a Teen Challenge construction project, Fritz grew increasingly agitated. Every man he saw standing idle drew his judgment. "If they'd just work harder," he muttered, "they could make it. My dad always said, 'Pull yourself up by your own bootstraps.'" His heart was cold toward the very people we'd come to serve.

That night, Fritz made a farmer's decision. Sleeping on our construction site's concrete slab would save travel time and let him start work at dawn. Practical and efficient—very Fritz.

But before sunrise, singing woke him. The Teen Challenge men—recovering addicts working to rebuild their lives

—had gathered for worship and prayer in the pre-dawn darkness. Were they "working hard" by Fritz's standard definition? No. They were doing something else entirely: crying out to God for freedom from addiction, singing through their pain, holding each other up through recovery.

When our team arrived hours later, we found Fritz in tears. "I've been such a fool," he said. "These men work harder than I ever have just to stay clean another day. Worshipping, praying ... I've never seen something so beautiful."

The temperature of his heart had completely changed. And with that warmth came an explosion of generosity. Fritz threw himself into the construction with renewed purpose, sharing with the men his talent for construction. He no longer saw lazy people in poverty; he saw fighters who needed someone with a warm heart and capable hands to come alongside them.

Look at how the Good Samaritan used his practical talents: "He bandaged his wounds, pouring on oil and wine. Then he put the man on his own donkey, brought him to an inn and took care of him" (Luke 10:34). No words recorded. No sermon preached. Just practical skill applied with compassion—knowing how to clean wounds with wine, soothe them with oil, and bandage it all with skill.

This is what guiding someone through transformation requires. As people work through being buried with Christ and raised to new life (Chapters 12 and 13), they need more than good theology. They need someone willing to share their practical talents.

Maybe you're a web developer who can help someone launch a recovery ministry online. Perhaps you're a business consultant who can help an ex-addict develop a business plan. Whatever your skill set—teacher, counselor, carpenter, social media strategist—when your heart is warmed, your talents become tools of transformation.

Fritz left North Dakota with callused hands, but he returned with a changed heart. And he left behind a group of men in Honduras who now knew how to lay bricks in a Fritz sort of way! More importantly—those men witnessed the compassion of Christ through the hands of a changed man.

What are your talents? How can you use them to bless others?

Time

Have you noticed? Everything we've explored so far —Testimony, Temperature, and Talent—all require one precious resource: Time.

The road from Jerusalem to Jericho wasn't a scenic route for pleasure. It was seventeen miles of desert—a brutal 4,000-foot drop in elevation over rocky terrain—with bandits hiding in caves. This route was functional. It was a necessary evil if you needed to get from one place to another. Most travelers would push through in a single day, especially if going downhill to Jericho.

The Samaritan had his day planned; he'd be in Jericho by nightfall ... then he saw the beaten man. Notice this easily missed detail: "He put the man on his own donkey, brought him to an inn and took care of him. The next day..." (Luke 10:34-35).

The next day.

Three words that reveal the true cost. The Samaritan's one-day journey became two. His schedule was disrupted, and his appointments in Jericho would have to wait. Whatever business drove him down that dangerous road —it all got pushed aside for a stranger's need.

This is a sobering truth about helping others become like Christ: transformation doesn't follow our timeline. You can't mentor someone through their "burial and resurrection" during a lunch break. (Nothing wrong with using your lunch break ... but it may take quite a few of them).

When someone's beaten up on life's roadside, they don't need your leftover minutes.

> They need your days.
> Probably your weeks.
> Quite often your years.

The Samaritan could have justified passing by:

> "I have commitments in Jericho."
> "Someone else with more time will come."
> "I'll help on my way back."

We know these excuses because we've used them. But love stops the clock. Compassion cancels appointments.

How will you carve out time in your weekly schedule to mentor someone in the Anchor of Becoming like Christ?

Treasure

The beaten man on the Jericho road needed more than empathy. If the Good Samaritan had simply knelt beside him and crooned "You've got a friend in me," the man would have died with a movie soundtrack playing in his head.[86]

Compassion doesn't pay medical bills. Only cash does. Look at what the Samaritan did:

> The next day he took out two denarii and gave them to the innkeeper. "Look after him," he said, "and when I return, I will reimburse you for any extra expense you may have. (Luke 10:35)

Two denarii is two days' wages. And here's what makes this remarkable—when you're traveling the bandit-infested road from Jerusalem to Jericho, you don't carry excess cash. You bring what you need, nothing more. Too much money makes you too tempting of a target. When the Samaritan handed over those two silver coins, he was likely giving away his own provisions for the journey. His gift to help meant he himself would hurt.

Sometimes that's exactly what transformation costs. For our investment in others to truly help them, it has to personally cost us.

Paul understood this principle. When a severe famine struck Jerusalem, he urged the churches he'd planted to move beyond feeling to funding. The Macedonian churches stunned him with their response:

> In the midst of a very severe trial, their

overflowing joy and their extreme poverty welled up in rich generosity. For I testify that they gave as much as they were able, and even beyond their ability. (2 Corinthians 8:2-3)

Catch that—their extreme poverty resulted in rich generosity. The Macedonians gave beyond their ability. Their gift was given at great cost to themselves so that others could be helped.

Paul used the testimony of the Macedonian church to challenge the Corinthian church:

But since you excel in everything—in faith, in speech, in knowledge, in complete earnestness and in the love we have kindled in you—see that you also excel in this grace of giving. (2 Corinthians 8:7)

To paraphrase Paul's words to the Corinthians, "You're great at blessing people with your Time, Talent, Testimony and Temperature. Now bless them with your Treasure."

American Christians could use this challenge. Despite our prosperity, charitable giving in the United States has flatlined at around 2 percent of our income for decades.[87] We feel deeply. We speak passionately. We share posts about injustice. But when someone beaten up by life needs actual help becoming whole again, we've tightened our purse strings.

Here's what I'm getting at. Discipling someone requires more than an open heart—it requires an open wallet. This might look like sponsoring counseling sessions, covering rent during someone's rehab, paying for kids to attend camp while their parents rebuild their marriage, tithing to your local church, setting up a recurring donation to support missionaries, or buying groceries for the family whose breadwinner isn't getting a paycheck because of the latest government shutdown.

The Samaritan made a promise before he left: "I will reimburse you for any extra expense." He didn't set a cap. He didn't say "up to a reasonable amount." He committed to whatever it took for complete restoration.

The road to becoming like Christ can be expensive—for others and for you. But I'm convinced it's a worthwhile investment. Jesus said:

> Give, and it will be given to you. A good measure, pressed down, shaken together and running over, will be poured into your lap. For with the measure you use, it will be measured to you. (Luke 6:38)

How has God blessed you? Are you willing to share your treasure, and "excel in this grace of giving"?

Ties

The Samaritan gave everything he had—Testimony, Temperature, Time, Talent, Treasure. But eventually, even he reached his limit.

After a full night of caring for the wounded stranger, morning came with a hard truth: his journey to Jericho couldn't wait any longer. Perhaps he had business obligations. Maybe family was expecting him. Whatever the reason, he had to go.

Did he leave the man helpless? No. He deployed his final resource: his Ties. "Look after him," he told the innkeeper (Luke 10:35). This simple request reveals something profound. The Samaritan had people who trusted him, and his network of relationships became the wounded man's safety net.

The early church modeled this beautifully:

> All the believers were together and had everything in common. They sold property and possessions to give to anyone who had need… And the Lord added to their number daily those who were being saved. (Acts 2:44-47)

Notice the phrase: "All the believers." Not one superhero Christian. Not a solo wealthy patron. A community, each contributing what they had, creating a network of transformational Ties.

Your Ties—friends, family, fellow travelers—multiply your impact exponentially. Maybe you can't provide counseling, but you know a therapist who offers sliding scale fees. Perhaps you can't teach job skills, but you know a business owner who is willing to train untrained workers. You might not have extra room in your home, but you're connected to someone who does.

This is how the kingdom works. We're not called to be anyone's everything—we're called to be faithful with what we have while connecting them to others who can provide what we can't.

A passage from Peter comes to mind:

> As you come to him, the living Stone—rejected

by humans but chosen by God and precious to him—you also, like living stones, are being built into a spiritual house to be a holy priesthood, offering spiritual sacrifices acceptable to God through Jesus Christ. (1 Peter 2:4–5)

You're one stone in a cathedral of living stones—a network of fellow Jesus-followers who are your potential partners in someone else's resurrection story.

How might God use your Ties to help another on their journey toward becoming like Christ?

Space In Your Resources

The Samaritan gave six things: Testimony, Temperature, Time, Talent, Treasure, and Ties. But really, he gave one thing—himself.

That Wednesday night in 1980, Commander Jake did the same. He gave me and the other boys more than plywood and paper. He gave us himself—his workplace, his resources, his time, his connections. He showed us what "go and do likewise" looks like with skin on it.

Who sees you as their Commander Jake?
Who sees you as their Good Samaritan?

As you create space for others to belong, believe, and ultimately become like Christ, I challenge you to be the kind of person who shares your story, feels what others feel, ignores the clock, gives of your skill, pays the bill, and creates meaningful connections.

Consider the Good Samaritan—then "go and do likewise."

Questions For Reflection

1. Remember a "Commander Jake" from your life—someone who invested their personal resources in your spiritual growth. Which of the six Ts (Testimony, Temperature, Time, Talent, Treasure, Ties) did they share with you? How did it impact your journey of becoming like Christ?

2. Of the six resources discussed, which is the most natural for you to share? Which feels most challenging or costly?

3. Think about someone in your life who might be "beaten up on the side of the road" right now—struggling with addiction, divorce, job loss, grief, or spiritual doubts. What specific resource from the six Ts do they most need? What would it look like for you to offer that this week?

4. Which relationship or community connection could you activate this week to multiply your impact, and what first step will you take?

5. Look at your calendar and bank account from the last month. Where did you invest your time and treasure? What story do these investments tell about your priorities? How might you create more margin in both areas to be available when God brings someone across your path who needs what you have to offer?

18. BELAYED TO BELAY

> *And the things you have heard me say in the presence of many witnesses entrust to reliable people who will also be qualified to teach others.* (2 Timothy 2:2)

I almost didn't write this final chapter—not because I didn't want to, but because I started slipping back into that well-worn modern path. I hate to admit it, but I nearly made the very mistake I warned about in Chapter 1.

In these last few chapters, I've talked about *you* being on belay.

> *You* on mission.
> *You* creating space at your table.
> *You* creating space in your conversations.
> *You* creating space in your resources.

But then what?

Is the goal to help people reach spiritual wholeness—where they've believed and become—just for maturity's sake? Please, no. That's exactly how we ended up with "Believe → Behave → Belong → Be Seated."

Here's what I nearly missed: being on belay isn't complete until you've helped others be on belay too—until you've empowered *them* to guide others along this same Anchored Path.

The journey we've rediscovered isn't: Belong → Believe → Become.

It's Belong → Believe → Become → *Belay* →

Remember Jesus's final command to His disciples? Make disciples. And what were those disciples supposed to do? Make more disciples. And those disciples? Make more disciples. We belay others to belay others to belay others … until we breathe our final breath or Jesus returns in glory.

Paul understood this relay race. From a Roman prison cell, knowing his time was nearly up, he wrote to Timothy, "I have fought the good fight, I have finished the race, I have kept the faith" (2 Timothy 4:7).

18. BELAYED TO BELAY

Figure 18.1

How did Paul know he had finished the race? He had passed the baton (figure 18.1):

> You then, my son, be strong in the grace that is in Christ Jesus. And the things you have heard me say in the presence of many witnesses entrust to reliable people who will also be qualified to teach others. (2 Timothy 2:1-2)

That's four generations in one verse: Paul to Timothy to reliable people to others. Do you see the beauty of this? It's worked for two millennia. Since the moment Jesus ascended, His followers have been belaying others—generation to generation—until someone belayed you.

Someone invited you to belong before you believed. Someone believed in you as you became. Someone belayed you into this moment.

Now it's your turn. Guide another along the Anchored Path, preparing them to lead others along the Anchored Path. Share the rope. Pass the baton. Help others belay.

Belong → Believe → Become → Belay →

Questions For Reflection

1. Who belayed you? Think back through your spiritual journey. Who invited you to belong before you believed? Who believed in you as you became? Take a moment to thank God for these people who passed the baton to you.

2. In what areas of ministry or service have you been trying to do everything yourself? What keeps you from inviting others to join you on mission?

3. Who is God calling you to equip? Look around your life right now. Who has God placed in your path that you could help guide from belonging to believing to becoming to belaying? Be specific—write down a name or two.

4. What's your next step? For the person(s) you just named, what's one practical thing you could do this week to help them take their next step along the path? How can you prepare them not just to follow Jesus, but to lead others to Him?

5. How does knowing maturity leads to mission—belaying others—reshape your faith and your involvement in ministry?

APPENDIX A: BELAYING AND ANCHORS

Belay: The Climbing Definition

In rock climbing, to belay means to manage and secure a climbing rope through a belay device, protecting the climber in the event of a fall.

The belayer—the person managing the rope—attaches the device to their own harness and passes the rope through it (figure A1). This allows the belayer to control the rope precisely and keep the climber safe. If the climber falls at any point, the belayer applies friction to the rope with the device, catching the climber before they hit the ground.

The beauty of belaying lies in its simplicity: one person below enables another to climb heights that would be impossible to do alone safely. The belayer doesn't climb; they serve. Their entire focus is on the other person's ascent.

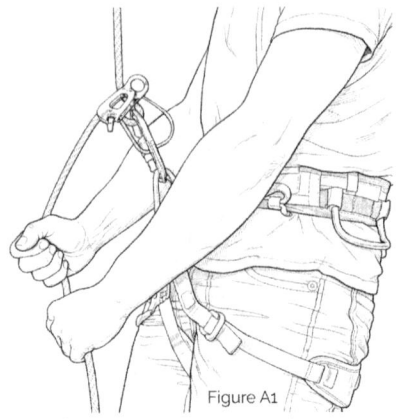

Figure A1

Essential Belay Commands

Climbers and belayers use specific commands for clear communication:

"On belay?" The climber asks if the belayer is ready and secured.

"Belay on!" The belayer confirms they're ready, and the climber is protected.

"Climbing!" The climber announces they're starting their ascent.

"Climb on!" The belayer acknowledges and gives permission to proceed.

"Off belay" The climber has reached safety and no longer needs protection.

"Take!" The climber asks the belayer to remove the slack and hold them on the rope.

"Lower!" The climber requests to be lowered in a controlled descent.

Belay: The Naval Definition

The term "belay" also appears in naval tradition, where it has two meanings. First, to secure a rope by winding it around a cleat or pin. Second, when a naval officer shouts, "Belay that order!" they're essentially saying, "Stop that!" or "Cancel the previous command."

Both uses of "belay" share the core concept of securing, holding fast, and providing stability.

Anchors: From Sea To Summit

Mountain climbing and sailing share another crucial term: anchor. Most people are familiar with a boat anchor —a heavy object attached to a rope or chain that moors a vessel to the seabed.

In climbing, an anchor serves a similar purpose. It's a secure point of attachment that bears the weight and force of the entire climbing system. The anchor is what keeps everyone safe. Without a solid anchor, even the best belayer cannot protect the climber.

Anchors can be natural features like sturdy trees or rock formations, or they can be manufactured equipment such as bolts or cams that are placed directly into the rock (figure A2).

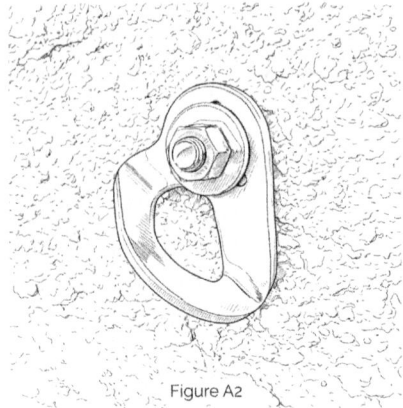
Figure A2

On Belay: Our Term For Being On Mission

When we say we're "on belay," we mean we're actively engaged in God's mission (Matthew 28:18-20)—not as bystanders but as servants supporting others in their spiritual ascent.

Living "on belay" takes many forms—from leading a small group to cleaning up after an event, from serving overseas to helping a neighbor across the street. Wherever we are and whatever we're doing, we're called to support others in their journey toward Jesus.

Four Anchors Of Growth In Christ

Throughout this book, we've explored four spiritual anchors that secure us in our journey along the Anchored Path:

Belong: The anchor of God's love and Christian community.

Believe: The anchor of repentance, faith, and

worship of Jesus.

Become: The anchor of burying the old life, being raised to new life, and receiving instruction for this process.

Belay: The anchor of being on mission with Jesus—serving, guiding, and mentoring others.

APPENDIX B: LISTENING PRAYER

Listening Guidelines

The following eight guidelines are from the ministry of the Navigators. This is a simple, repeatable practice for quieting yourself and attending to God's voice.

1. Come fully present before God.

   Fix your attention fully on Jesus and away from distractions.

   "Fixing our eyes on Jesus, the pioneer and perfecter of faith" (Hebrews 12:2).

2. Exercise Christ's authority over all other voices.

   Pray similar to, "In the name of Jesus Christ, I command all other voices to be silent."

   "Submit yourselves, then, to God. Resist the devil, and he will flee from you" (James 4:7).

3. Ask the Three-in-One to reveal Himself in a special way.

   "Hasten, O God, to save me; come quickly, Lord, to help me" (Psalm 70:1).

4. Ask God to search your heart.

Talk to Him about what He reveals, confess any known sin.

"Search me, God, and know my heart; test me and know my anxious thoughts. See if there is any offensive way in me, and lead me in the way everlasting" (Psalm 139:23–24).

5. Ask Jesus to communicate with you.

"The Lord came and stood there, calling as at the other times, 'Samuel! Samuel!' Then Samuel said, 'Speak, for your servant is listening'" (1 Samuel 3:10).

"I have much more to say to you, more than you can now bear. But when he, the Spirit of truth, comes, he will guide you into all the truth. He will not speak on his own; he will speak only what he hears, and he will tell you what is yet to come. He will glorify me because it is from me that he will receive what he will make known to you" (John 16:12–14).

6. Wait in silence.

"Truly my soul finds rest in God; my salvation comes from him" (Psalm 62:1).

"He says, 'Be still, and know that I am God; I will be exalted among the nations, I will be exalted in the earth'" (Psalm 46:10).

7. Write down impressions.

Usually this will be thoughts, pictures, or Scripture that enters your heart and mind.

> "These are the things God has revealed to us by his Spirit. The Spirit searches all things, even the deep things of God. For who knows a person's thoughts except their own spirit within them? In the same way no one knows the thoughts of God except the Spirit of God. What we have received is not the spirit of the world, but the Spirit who is from God, so that we may understand what God has freely given us. This is what we speak, not in words taught us by human wisdom but in words taught by the Spirit, explaining spiritual realities with Spirit-taught words. The person without the Spirit does not accept the things that come from the Spirit of God but considers them foolishness, and cannot understand them because they are discerned only through the Spirit. The person with the Spirit makes judgments about all things, but such a person is not subject to merely human judgments, for, 'Who has known the mind of the Lord so as to instruct him?' But we have the mind of Christ" (1 Corinthians 2:10–16).

8. Test impressions with God's word, His character and the body of Christ.

> Don't suppress the Spirit or stifle God's communication, but at the same time don't be gullible. Check it carefully with the Bible; keep only what passes the test.

> "Do not quench the Spirit. Do not treat prophecies with contempt but test them all; hold on to what is good, reject every kind of

evil" (1 Thessalonians 5:19–22).

Listening Questions

Here are the seven practical questions from Chapter 14 to guide your listening. Find a quiet place, ask one or two at a time, then listen. Journal what word, picture, or impression the Spirit brings:

1. *Jesus, what do You see when You look at me?*

    See yourself through God's eyes.

    "Jesus looked at him and loved him" (Mark 10:21).

2. *Is there anything I'm carrying that You want me to release?*

    Receive His freedom from your burdens.

    "Come to me, all who are weary and burdened, and I will give you rest" (Matthew 11:28).

3. *What are You inviting me into this season?*

    During this time of your life, open your heart to His direction.

    "My sheep listen to my voice; I know them, and they follow me" (John 10:27).

4. *Do You have a word or picture for me in this season?*

    God often speaks through images and metaphors.

    "Your word is a lamp to my feet and a light to my

path" (Psalm 119:105).

5. *What brings You joy when You think of me?*

   Discover His delight in you.

   "The Lord your God is with you, the Mighty Warrior who saves. He will take great delight in you; in his love he will no longer rebuke you, but will rejoice over you with singing" (Zephaniah 3:17).

6. *Is anything grieving Your heart right now?*

   Join Jesus in His compassion.

   "When he saw the crowds, he had compassion on them, because they were harassed and helpless, like sheep without a shepherd" (Matthew 9:36).

7. *How do You want me to join You today?*

   Listen for practical ways to partner with Him right now.

   "Whatever you did for one of the least of these brothers and sisters of mine, you did for me" (Matthew 25:40).

APPENDIX C: SCRIPTURAL DECLARATIONS

Four acrostics—REPENT, FAITH, BURIED, and RAISED—walk us through the Believe and Become Anchors: turning from sin, trusting Jesus, letting go of the old life, and stepping into our new identity in Christ.

The following scriptural declarations are meant to help you align your heart and mind with that journey. They are adapted from God's Word and written for you to personally declare truth over your life.

Read them slowly. Pray them out loud. Come back to them often. Let these words shape your thinking, direct your habits, and strengthen your walk with Jesus.

R.E.P.E.N.T.

Repentance marks the initial movement of believing in Christ. These declarations guide you through acknowledging sin, experiencing genuine sorrow, and embracing God's transformative grace. This is where lasting change begins.

Recognize Your Sin

> *There is a way that seems right to me, but in the end, it leads to death (Proverbs 14:12).*
>
> *I have sinned and fallen short of God's glory (Romans 3:23).*
>
> *Against You, Lord, I have sinned (Psalm 51:3–4).*

Experience Godly Sorrow

> *Godly sorrow brings repentance that leads me to salvation and leaves no regret (2 Corinthians 7:10).*
>
> *I humble myself before the Lord, and He lifts me up (James 4:10).*
>
> *God does not despise my broken and contrite heart (Psalm 51:17).*

Pray for Forgiveness

> *I confess my sins, and God is faithful and just to forgive and cleanse me (1 John 1:9).*
>
> *God has mercy on me according to His unfailing love (Psalm 51:1).*
>
> *God creates in me a pure heart and renews a steadfast spirit within me (Psalm 51:10).*

Embrace Making Amends

> *I look not only to my own interests, but also to the*

interests of others (Philippians 2:4).

If someone has something against me, I go and make it right (Matthew 5:23-24).

I do to others as I would have them do to me (Luke 6:31).

Nurture New Fruit

I bear fruit in keeping with repentance (Matthew 3:8).

I walk by the Spirit, and I will not gratify the desires of the flesh (Galatians 5:16).

The fruit of the Spirit is growing in my life —love, joy, peace, patience, kindness, goodness, faithfulness, gentleness and self-control (Galatians 5:22-23).

Thank God

I give thanks to the Lord, for He is good; His love endures forever (Psalm 107:1).

My soul blesses the Lord and remembers all His benefits—He forgives all my sins (Psalm 103:2-3).

Thanks be to God, who gives me the victory through our Lord Jesus Christ (1 Corinthians 15:57).

F.A.I.T.H.

Faith is the second movement in believing in Christ. These declarations help strengthen your trust in Him, moving beyond mere intellectual belief to active, living faith that shapes every aspect of life.

Factual

God's eternal power and divine nature are clearly seen in creation (Romans 1:20).

God exists, and he rewards me as I earnestly seek him (Hebrews 11:6).

The Word became flesh, lived among us, died for my sins, was buried, and rose again (John 1:14, 1 Corinthians 15:3–4).

Actual

As for me and my household, we will serve the Lord (Joshua 24:15).

Faith is confidence in what I hope for and assurance about what I do not yet see (Hebrews 11:1).

I live by faith in the Son of God, who loved me and gave Himself for me (Galatians 2:20).

If You Confess

I declare with my mouth, "Jesus is Lord," and believe in my heart God raised Him from the dead (Romans 10:9–10).

I confess Jesus is the Son of God; God lives in me and I in Him (1 John 4:15).

My mouth speaks what my heart is full of (Matthew 12:34).

Together With

My faith and deeds work together—I show my faith by what I do (James 2:18, 22).

I love Jesus and do what He says (Luke 6:46).

My faith expresses itself through love (Galatians 5:6).

Habitual

Just as I received Christ Jesus as Lord, I continue to live in Him (Colossians 2:6).

I take up my cross daily and follow Jesus (Luke 9:23).

I follow in His steps (1 Peter 2:21).

B.U.R.I.E.D.

Being buried with Christ means letting go of our old life. These declarations help you identify and release the things that need to die so that new life can emerge.

Brokenness and Pain

The Lord heals my broken heart and binds up my wounds (Psalm 147:3).

The Lord comforts me in all my troubles (2 Corinthians 1:4).

I call to God for help and He heals me (Psalm 30:2).

Unforgiveness

I forgive those who hurt me; they do not know what they are doing (Luke 23:34).

I do not hold their sin against them (Acts 7:60).

I do good to those who hate me, bless those who

curse me, and pray for those who mistreat me (Luke 6:27-28).

Reign of Sin

I died with Christ, died to the power of sin's reign, and am no longer a slave to sin (Romans 6:1-6).

I have been redeemed and forgiven of all my sins (Colossians 1:14).

I have been crucified with Christ and I no longer live, but Christ lives in me (Galatians 2:20).

Idolatry

I keep myself from idols (1 John 5:21).

I flee from idolatry (1 Corinthians 10:14).

I have no other gods but God (Exodus 20:3).

Embarrassment

I believe in Jesus. I will not be put to shame (Romans 10:11).

God changes my shame into praise (Zephaniah 3:19).

I look to Him and am radiant; my face is never covered with shame (Psalm 34:5).

Deception

I renounce secret and shameful ways (2 Corinthians 4:2).

I submit to God and resist the devil; he flees from me (James 4:7).

I know the truth and it sets me free (John 8:32).

R.A.I.S.E.D.

Being raised with Christ is about embracing your new identity and purpose. These declarations help you walk confidently in who God says you are and what He's called you to do.

Relationship with God

I am God's child (John 1:12).

I am Jesus's friend (John 15:15).

I am a member of God's household (Ephesians 2:19).

Authority in Christ

I am born of God, and the devil cannot harm me (1 John 5:18).

I have access to God through His Spirit (Ephesians 2:18).

I may approach God's throne with confidence (Hebrews 4:16).

Inheritance

I am a co-heir with Christ (Romans 8:17).

I have been blessed with every spiritual blessing (Ephesians 1:3).

I have an inheritance that can never perish, spoil or fade; it is kept in heaven for me (1 Peter 1:4).

Sainthood

I am a saint (1 Corinthians 1:2; Ephesians 1:1; Philippians 1:1; Colossians 1:2).

I am a new creation (2 Corinthians 5:17).

I have been justified—completely forgiven and made righteous (Romans 5:1).

Embark on a Mission

I am the salt of the earth and the light of the world (Matthew 5:13-14).

I am chosen and appointed by Christ to bear fruit (John 15:16).

I am created in Christ Jesus to do good works (Ephesians 2:10).

Disciple Others

What I've received, I pass on to others—so they can pass it on too (2 Timothy 2:2).

God has given me the ministry of reconciliation (2 Corinthians 5:18).

I am sent to make disciples of all nations (Matthew 28:19).

Living These Truths

These declarations aren't meant to be a one-time exercise, but rather a continuous path of transformation. Return to them regularly—perhaps focusing on one section per week or month.

APPENDIX C: SCRIPTURAL DECLARATIONS

As you declare these truths, you'll find them becoming more than words on a page; they'll become the very fabric of your daily walk with Christ. Let them guide your prayers, shape your decisions, and strengthen your faith as you continue to walk the Anchored Path.

APPENDIX D: ANCHORED ORIGINS

The four Anchors of the Anchored Path are not new —they're just a memorable way to visualize Jesus's two Great Statements, and four primary Purposes that flow from them (figure D1):

The Great Commandment:

> Jesus replied: "'Love the Lord your God with all your heart and with all your soul and with all your mind.' This is the first and greatest commandment. And the second is like it: 'Love your neighbor as yourself.' All the Law and the Prophets hang on these two commandments." (Matthew 22:37–40)

The Great Commission:

> Then Jesus came to them and said, "All authority

in heaven and on earth has been given to me. Therefore go and make disciples of all nations, baptizing them in the name of the Father and of the Son and of the Holy Spirit, and teaching them to obey everything I have commanded you. And surely I am with you always, to the very end of the age." (Matthew 28:18-20)

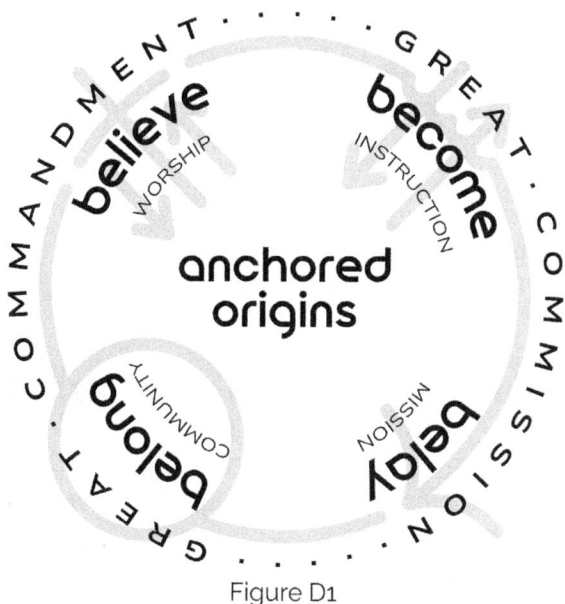

Figure D1

2 Greats Articulate 4 Purposes

In these two Great Statements, we find four primary Purposes for the church and every follower of Jesus.

Community: "Love your neighbor as yourself" (Great Commandment).

Worship: "Love the Lord your God with all your heart" (Great Commandment).

Instruction: "Obey everything I have commanded you" (Great Commission).

Mission: "Go and make disciples of all nations" (Great Commission).

4 Anchors Alliterate 4 Purposes

The four Anchors are simply a mnemonic device to help us remember the four Purposes.

Belong: our term for "Community."

Believe: our term for "Worship."

Become: our term for "Instruction."

Belay: our term for "Mission."

Anchored Communities And Christians

From these *Greats, Purposes,* and *Anchors,* we can arrive at helpful definitions for an *Anchored Community* and an *Anchored Christian:*

Anchored Community (figure D2): A hospitable community (Belong/Community) of Jesus-worshipers (Believe/Worship), growing in faith (Become/Instruction) and on mission with Him (Belay/Mission).

Anchored Christian (figure D3): A hospitable (Belong/Community) Jesus-worshiper (Believe/Worship), growing in faith (Become/Instruction) and on mission with Him (Belay/Mission).

APPENDIX D: ANCHORED ORIGINS

Figure D2

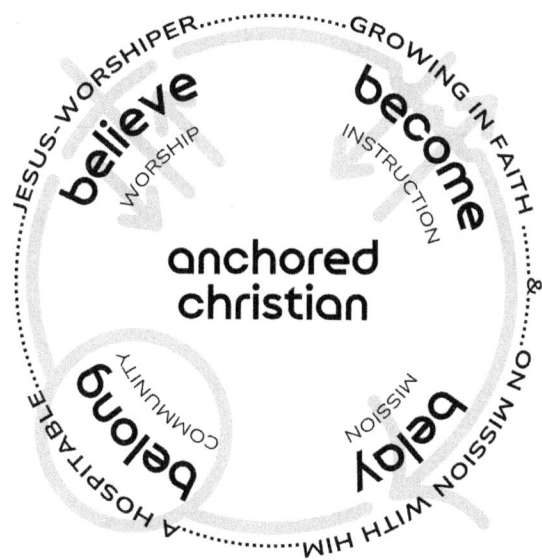

Figure D3

APPENDIX E: ANCHORED STAGES

In this book, I've invited the willing reader to walk the Anchored Path of following Jesus—a journey marked by four Anchors: Belong, Believe, Become, and Belay.

It may also be helpful to articulate this path with eight more granular stages (figure E1) which spell out ANCHORED: Against, Not-Against, Convicted, Happy, Obedient, Refining, Engaged, and Discipler.

APPENDIX E: ANCHORED STAGES

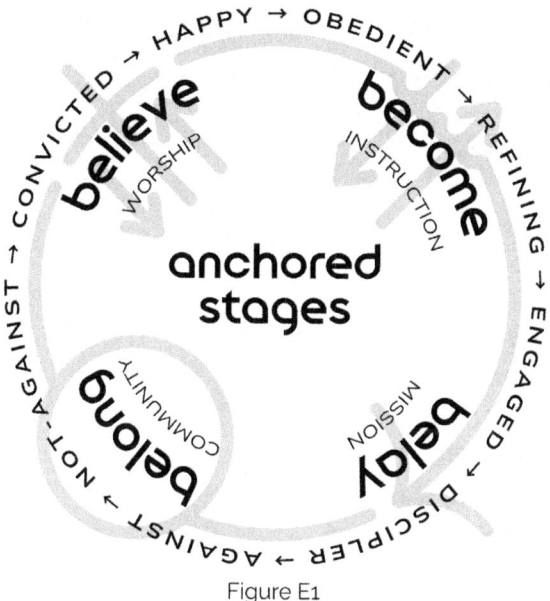

Figure E1

How To Use These Stages

The Stages of the Anchored Path serve as both a mirror and a map:

For Your Own Journey:

Prayerfully consider where you currently are on this path. Then look at the next Stage and ask, "What specific steps could I take to grow forward?" Remember, spiritual growth isn't always linear; you might find yourself circling back to and doubling up on a few stages as you deepen your faith.

For Guiding Others:

As you walk alongside someone in their faith journey, use this path to help them identify what Stage they are in and what they might need next. Rather than pushing them to skip ahead, meet them where they are and gently encourage the next faithful step.

Next Steps:

Ask, "What is needed to help me or someone I'm guiding move from one Stage to the next?"

> Against to Not-Against
> Not-Against to Convicted
> Convicted to Happy
> Happy to Obedient
> Obedient to Refining
> Refining to Engaged
> Engaged to Discipler

The Anchored Stages

Here are the Anchored Stages along with their definitions using the Apostle Paul's life and words as an example. (Note: Paul was called Saul before his conversion).

Against (God)

> A person who is antagonistic toward faith in Jesus.

> "Meanwhile, Saul was still breathing out murderous threats against the Lord's disciples. He went to the high priest and asked him for letters to the synagogues in Damascus, so that if he found any there who belonged to the Way, whether men or women, he might take them as prisoners to Jerusalem" (Acts 9:1–2).

Not-Against (God)

A person who isn't following Jesus but is also not hostile—they're open to spiritual conversations and willing to explore faith.

"As [Paul] neared Damascus on his journey, suddenly a light from heaven flashed around him. He fell to the ground and heard a voice say to him, 'Saul, Saul, why do you persecute me?' 'Who are you, Lord?' Saul asked. 'I am Jesus, whom you are persecuting,' he replied" (Acts 9:3–5).

Convicted (of Sin)

A person who recognizes their need for God and feels the weight of sin but hasn't fully understood the solution.

Paul writes in Romans, "For I know that good itself does not dwell in me, that is, in my sinful nature. For I have the desire to do what is good, but I cannot carry it out. For I do not do the good I want to do, but the evil I do not want to do—this I keep on doing ... What a wretched man I am! Who will rescue me from this body that is subject to death?" (Romans 7:18–19, 24).

Happy (Blessed and Favored through Salvation)

A person who has repented of sin and placed their faith in Jesus Christ.

Paul writes in Romans, "Blessed and happy and favored are those whose lawless acts have been forgiven, and whose sins have been covered up and completely buried. Blessed and happy and favored is the man whose sin the Lord will not take into account nor charge against him" (Romans 4:7–8, AMP).

Obedient (to God)

A believer who is learning to hear and obey the leading of the Holy Spirit, with one of the first acts of obedience being baptism.

"Then Ananias went to the house and entered it. Placing his hands on Saul, he said, 'Brother Saul, the Lord—Jesus, who appeared to you on the road as you were coming here—has sent me so that you may see again and be filled with the Holy Spirit.' Immediately, something like scales fell from Saul's eyes, and he could see again. He got up and was baptized" (Acts 9:17–18).

When speaking with the King, Paul says, "So then, King Agrippa, I was not disobedient to the vision from heaven" (Acts 26:19).

Refining (Learning, Growing, and Becoming)

A believer actively learning to bury their old life while embracing their new identity as a child of God.

Paul writes in Romans, "What shall we say, then? Shall we go on sinning so that grace may increase? By no means! We are those who have died to sin; how can we live in it any longer? Or don't you know that all of us who were baptized into Christ Jesus were baptized into his death?

We were therefore buried with him through baptism into death in order that, just as Christ was raised from the dead through the glory of the Father, we too may live a new life" (Romans 6:1–4).

Engaged (in Ministry and Service)

A believer engaged in discovering their gifts and serving others in love.

Paul writes in Galatians, "You, my brothers and sisters, were called to be free. But do not use your freedom to indulge the flesh; rather, serve one another humbly in love. For the entire law is fulfilled in keeping this one command: 'Love your neighbor as yourself'" (Galatians 5:13–14).

Discipler (of Others)

A believer who makes disciples who make disciples, reproducing the Anchored Path of Belong, Believe, Become, and Belay in others.

Paul writes to Timothy, "And the things you have heard me say in the presence of many witnesses entrust to reliable people who will also be qualified to teach others" (2 Timothy 2:2).

Keep In Mind:

The Anchored Path isn't a rigid formula but a helpful guide. The Holy Spirit works uniquely in each person's life, and some may move through these Stages in different ways or at different paces. The goal isn't speed but steady growth toward becoming an anchored follower of Jesus who guides others along the same Anchored Path.

[1] Read the whole story in Preston Ulmer, *The Doubters Club* (Colorado Springs, CO: David C Cook, 2021).

[2] See https://nextwave.community/

[3] In Mandarin Chinese, the name for China is 中国 (Zhōngguó), which literally means "Middle Country."

[4] Jeffrey M. Jones, "U.S. Church Membership Falls Below Majority for First Time," *Gallup*, March 29, 2021. https://news.gallup.com/poll/341963/church-membership-falls-below-majority-first-time.aspx

[5] Church Dropouts Have Risen to 64%—But What About Those Who Stay?" *Barna Group*. Accessed October 30, 2025. https://www.barna.com/research/resilient-disciples/

[6] Emo Philips, "Britain's Favourite Religious Joke," *The Guardian*, September 29, 2005. https://www.theguardian.com/stage/2005/sep/29/comedy.religion

[7] Scriptural examples of prevenient grace include: "… God's kindness is intended to lead you to repentance" (Romans 2:4), "For the grace of God has appeared that offers salvation to all people" (Titus 2:11), and "The true light that gives light to everyone was coming into the world" (John 1:9).

[8] That might sound a bit pretentious, I know. So, here's a couple things to know about people who live in Colorado. First, we all think we're "native Coloradans" even if we've only lived here a short while. Second, we think we're the only people with "real" mountains. But honestly—deep down—most of us know we're not truly locals, and we also know that many other places in the world have very nice mountains. (Don't tell anyone from Colorado I told you this).

[9] See Appendix A for a full definition of belaying and anchoring.

[10] Henri J. M. Nouwen, *Life of the Beloved: Spiritual Living in a Secular World* (New York: Crossroad, 1992), 30.

[11] Eugene H. Peterson, *Run with the Horses: The Quest for Life at Its Best* (Downers Grove, IL: InterVarsity Press, 1983), 120.

[12] 1 John 4:19, KJV.

[13] This is true of the most popular, trusted translations of the Bible such as the NIV, KJV, ESV, NLT, HCSB, MSG, NASB, NRS, ASV, and RSV.

[14] The word parable comes from the Greek and means "to set beside" or "to compare"—essentially, comparing or setting a familiar

story beside a spiritual truth. Gerhard Kittel and Gerhard Friedrich, eds., *Theological Dictionary of the New Testament*, trans. Geoffrey W. Bromiley, vol. 5 (Grand Rapids, MI: Eerdmans, 1967), 744–813, s.v. "παραβολή (parabolē)."

[15] This interpretation has roots in early Christian writings, including Origen's *Homilies on Luke*, Clement of Alexandria's *Stromata*, and Augustine's *Quaestiones Evangeliorum*.

[16] We'll return to this primary point in Chapter 17: Space With Our Resources, where we'll see how the Good Samaritan's costly use of six resources (testimony, temperature, talent, time, treasure, and ties) becomes our model for investing in others' transformation.

[17] "I have no husband," she replied. Jesus said to her, "You are right when you say you have no husband. The fact is, you have had five husbands, and the man you now have is not your husband. What you have just said is quite true" (John 4:17–18).

[18] See John 4:1-42 for the whole conversation.

[19] See John 3:1-21 for the whole conversation.

[20] See Acts 9:1-19 for Paul's story.

[21] Zòngzi (粽子, pronounced zòngzi) are traditional Chinese rice dumplings made of glutinous rice stuffed with fillings such as sweet red bean paste, pork, or egg yolk. They are wrapped in bamboo or reed leaves, tied with string, and steamed or boiled. Zòngzi are especially associated with the Dragon Boat Festival (端午节, Duānwǔ Jié), which commemorates the poet Qu Yuan.

[22] Michael Frost, *Surprise the World* (NavPress, 2016), 44. Frost attributes this insight to Tim Chester, *A Meal with Jesus* (Crossway, 2011).

[23] Robert J. Karris, *Eating Your Way through Luke's Gospel* (Collegeville, MN: Liturgical Press, 2006), 14.

[24] Interesting fact: Jesus and His disciples likely ate around a triclinium—a U-shaped table where guests reclined on couches, common in ancient Jewish and Roman dining. Practically, it allowed people to look at each other (like when sitting at a circular table), but the open side of the U allowed servers to bring food to the guests.

[25] Bono, interviewed by Michka Assayas in *Bono: In Conversation with Michka Assayas* (New York: Riverhead Books, 2005), 227.

[26] C. S. Lewis, *The Weight of Glory and Other Addresses* (New York:

Harper One, 2001), 140.

[27] Acts 20:21.

[28] Exodus 20.

[29] "Love the LORD your God with all your heart and with all your soul and with all your strength" (Deuteronomy 6:5).

[30] "Do not seek revenge or bear a grudge against anyone among your people, but love your neighbor as yourself. I am the LORD" (Leviticus 19:18).

[31] "We are therefore Christ's ambassadors, as though God were making his appeal through us. We implore you on Christ's behalf: Be reconciled to God" (2 Corinthians 5:20).

[32] We've seen this verse a few times in this book, but here we finally look at the entire verse.

[33] See Galatians 3:24 and Romans 3:19-20.

[34] See 2 Samuel 12:10.

[35] I say "at least" because we also tried to teach them to specify what they were sorry for: "I'm sorry *I pinched* you ... will you forgive me?" "I'm sorry for *wrecking your toy* ... will you forgive me?"

[36] "Let us then approach God's throne of grace with confidence, so that we may receive mercy and find grace to help us in our time of need" (Hebrews 4:16).

[37] Thomas Watson, *The Doctrine of Repentance* (Edinburgh: Banner of Truth Trust, 1987), 19.

[38] You can find more helpful scriptural declarations like these in Appendix C.

[39] See John 3:3-8.

[40] This book isn't meant to defend this statement in detail, but if you're interested in the historical evidence for Jesus's life, death, and resurrection, I recommend a deeper dive into resources like *Evidence That Demands a Verdict* by Josh McDowell, or *Mere Christianity* by C.S. Lewis.

[41] This statement was inspired by David Pawson in *The Normal Christian Birth* (Guildford, UK: Anchor Recordings, 1989), 31, where he writes, "It is a truism that faith is based on facts, not on feelings. But it cannot be repeated too often, especially in an existential culture where subjective experience is regarded as the touchstone of reality."

[42] C. S. Lewis, *Mere Christianity* (New York: Macmillan, 1952), 40–

41. In all editions, this appears in Book II, Chapter 3, "The Shocking Alternative."

[43] This statement was inspired by Pawson in *The Normal Christian Birth*, 34, where he writes, "Christian faith is believing in a single person rather than a series of propositions. It is not just believing that Jesus died and rose again; it is believing in the Jesus who died and rose again. The change of preposition is crucial, transferring faith from the mind, where it rightly begins, to the will (which is the citadel of our personality and very close to what the Bible means by 'heart'). It is a shift from the objective (information about Jesus) to the subjective (confidence in Jesus). Whereas in the previous section we highlighted the danger of a subjective faith without any objective content, we must now be aware of the opposite peril!"

[44] Admittedly, I have met a few people who say they enjoy the smell of coffee as it's roasting. Personally, I think they're just anticipating the end result and have convinced themselves that the roasting smell is pleasant.

[45] You can find more helpful scriptural declarations like these in Appendix C.

[46] Max Lucado, *Just Like Jesus* (Nashville: Word Publishing, 1998), 13.

[47] Neil T. Anderson, *Victory Over the Darkness: Realizing the Power of Your Identity in Christ* (Minneapolis, MN: Bethany House, 2019), 71.

[48] Philippians 3:12-14.

[49] Some ancient manuscripts do not include verse 37, so modern translations like the NIV place it in a footnote. I've italicized it and kept it in the main text here because these words—"If you believe with all your heart, you may" and "I believe that Jesus Christ is the Son of God"—beautifully capture the confession of faith that precedes baptism.

[50] Pawson, *The Normal Christian Birth*, 56.

[51] John Calvin, *Institutes of the Christian Religion*, trans. Henry Beveridge (Peabody, MA: Hendrickson Publishers, 2008), 108 (1.11.8).

[52] Marcus Warner, *A Deeper Walk* (DeKalb, IL: Deeper Walk International, 2019), 62.

[53] Warner, *A Deeper Walk*, 68.

[54] You can find more helpful scriptural declarations like these in

Appendix C.

[55] Anderson, *Victory Over the Darkness*, 55.

[56] This is the 13 character prayer I prayed: 头晕走，治愈来，奉耶稣的名，阿门。

[57] Anderson, *Victory Over the Darkness*, 47.

[58] Bill Gaither and Gloria Gaither, "Sinner Saved by Grace," performed by the Gaither Vocal Band, on *A Few Good Men* (Word Records, 1988).

[59] Anderson, *Victory Over the Darkness*, 49.

[60] Alan Hirsch and Debra Hirsch, *Untamed: Reactivating a Missional Form of Discipleship* (Grand Rapids, MI: Baker Books, 2010), 33.

[61] Michael Frost, *Surprise the World* (NavPress, 2016), 14.

[62] You can find more helpful scriptural declarations like these in Appendix C.

[63] Dallas Willard, *The Allure of Gentleness: Defending the Faith in the Manner of Jesus* (New York: Harper One, 2015), 104.

[64] Lewis, *Mere Christianity*, 131.

[65] 2 Corinthians 5:14-15.

[66] This is written from the perspective of my twelve-year-old self, who understood things in simple, painful terms. In reality, the settlement was more nuanced—my parents split the profit from the eventual sale of the home, and while Mom received most of the furnishings, she left behind essentials for Dad and my brother and me to use.

[67] We attended a counseling retreat at Alongside in Richland, MI. Visit https://www.alongsidecares.net for more information.

[68] I later learned that my dad was legally not allowed to be at the house that day.

[69] Rusty Rustenbach, *A Guide for Listening and Inner-Healing Prayer: Meeting God in the Broken Places* (Colorado Springs: NavPress, 2012).

[70] I've repeated these questions in Appendix B for your convenience.

[71] Matthew 5:1-7:29

[72] Anne Fishel, quoted in Jill Anderson, "The Benefit of Family Mealtime," *Harvard EdCast*, Harvard Graduate School of Education, April 8, 2020, https://www.gse.harvard.edu/ideas/edcast/20/04/benefit-family-mealtime

[73] I've written a book based on this story. It's an allegory titled *When Jesus Stole My Bread*, and it teaches us how to live at the intersection of truth and grace.

[74] There may be a bit of hyperbole here ... but we did end up with about twice as many people as originally planned.

[75] Epicurus, quoted in Diogenes Laertius, *Lives of Eminent Philosophers*, trans. R. D. Hicks (Cambridge, MA: Harvard University Press, 1925), 10.118.

[76] Michael Frost, *Surprise the World* (NavPress, 2016), 47.

[77] César Chávez, quoted in *César Chávez: An Organizer's Tale*, by Jacques E. Levy (New York: W. W. Norton, 2007), 62.

[78] There's nothing wrong with this approach; in fact, I believe there's a time and place for it. Sometimes that direct question is exactly what someone needs to hear.

[79] Dale Carnegie, *How to Win Friends and Influence People* (New York: Simon & Schuster, 1936), 78.

[80] The Story of the Good Samaritan is found in Luke 10:25–37.

[81] Details of Peng Yu's 2006 court case summarized from *Wikipedia*, "Xu Shoulan v. Peng Yu," https://en.wikipedia.org/wiki/Xu_Shoulan_v._Peng_Yu

[82] Information on China's 2017 Good Samaritan law summarized from *Wikipedia*, "Good Samaritan Law," https://en.wikipedia.org/wiki/Good_Samaritan_law

[83] Randy Newman, "You've Got a Friend in Me," from *Toy Story: An Original Walt Disney Records Soundtrack* (Burbank, CA: Walt Disney Records, 1995).

[84] Michael Skloff and Allee Willis, "I'll Be There for You," performed by The Rembrandts, on *Friends Original TV Soundtrack* (New York: Reprise Records, 1995).

[85] Gary Portnoy and Judy Hart-Angelo, "Where Everybody Knows Your Name," performed by Gary Portnoy, on *Cheers: Original Television Soundtrack* (Los Angeles: Gary Portnoy Music, 1982).

[86] This also would have been quite anachronistic since the song wouldn't come out for another 2000 years!

[87] Ben Gose, "The Stubborn 2% Giving Rate," *The Chronicle of Philanthropy*, June 16, 2016. https://www.philanthropy.com/news/the-stubborn-2-giving-rate/

ACKNOWLEDGEMENT

I want to offer special thanks to a few friends and family who supported me as I wrote *The Anchored Path*.

To Patty, your steady encouragement means the world to me. I couldn't have done this without your love, prayers, and support. I look forward to hiking many more paths with you.

To my dad, the first person I ever hiked with. The times we spent camping in the national parks were formational for me in so many ways. Thank you for asking, "When are you going to write another book?" It took some time, but here it is!

To Hallie, thank you for your keen eye, thoughtful questions, hours of reading, and honest feedback. This book is much stronger because of your input.

To Steve, thank you for writing the foreword, your mentorship, and your friendship. Much of what's here is the result of our conversations, your writing, and the meaningful work you've done through Urban Islands and the Next Wave Community. I wish every church planter could sit under your leadership and influence.

To Kevan, your questions and reflections pushed me to

think more deeply. A lot of what ended up in these pages was shaped by our conversations. I appreciate you.

To Christian, thank you for reminding us that every person has value and purpose. You've helped convince me of one of the foundational beliefs behind this book—that people can belong before they believe.

To all of Belay, thank you for sticking with me as I preached through these chapters. Before anyone else, this book is really for you!

And to you, the reader, I'm so grateful you've spent time with me on *The Anchored Path.* If you believe others should know about it, one of the best ways you can help is by leaving a review on Amazon, Goodreads, or wherever you talk about books. Thank you.

ABOUT THE AUTHOR

Paul Durbin

Paul Durbin is the founding pastor of Belay Church in Boulder, Colorado, where he and his wife Patty have been helping people walk the Anchored Path since 2019.

Paul's ministry began in the Midwest, where he served as a pastor for ten years—first as a youth pastor, then as lead pastor. He holds a bachelor's degree in International Studies and Biblical Studies from Trinity Bible College in Ellendale, North Dakota.

In 2008, Paul and Patty followed God's call to China, beginning an eleven-year adventure. After studying Mandarin in western China, Paul taught intercultural communication, speech, and English at a university in southern China. For the final six years, he pastored an International church in northern China, learning to lead across cultural and denominational lines.

Paul and Patty have four kids who have grown up across continents, campsites, and a home that's often full of guests. When Paul's not preaching, writing, or meeting someone for coffee, he's likely on a trail with his family or restoring an old camper.

The Durbins live at the base of the Rockies with a steady stream of guests who know there's always room for one more at the table.

Visit www.pauldurbin.co for contact information.

THE ANCHORED PATH

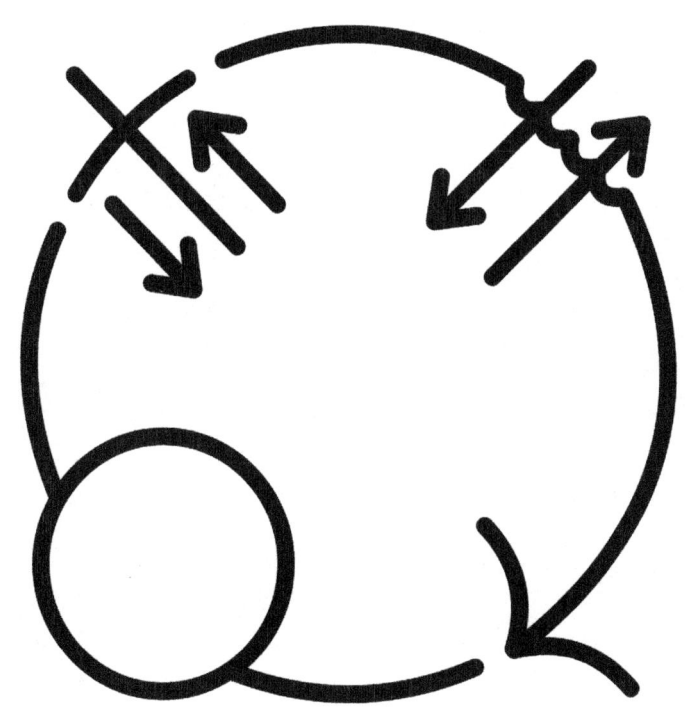

Printed in Dunstable, United Kingdom

78595692R00147